Guidance for Religious

GERALD KELLY, S.J.

Guidance

for Religious

Rev. John G. Donahue

NP

The Newman Press

WESTMINSTER, MARYLAND

1957

Second Printing 1957
Third Printing 1958

Imprimi potest: D. H. CONWAY, S.J.
     Provincial, Missouri Province
     January 23, 1956

Nihil obstat: EDWARD A. CERNY, S.S., D.D.
     Censor Librorum

Imprimatur: FRANCIS P. KEOUGH, D.D.
     Archbishop of Baltimore
     September 18, 1956

Contents

[v]

PART IV: *Guidance by Religious*

Religious and Spiritual Direction

THE first three sections of this book are intended as helps in the spiritual direction of religious. A brief discussion of the meaning of spiritual direction will explain this statement.

Spiritual direction may be defined as "instruction and encouragement of individuals on the way of perfection." Thus understood—and this is its primary meaning—it implies a personal relationship between two individuals. Its purpose is to help an individual attain the degree of perfection to which God is calling *him*. It supposes, therefore, that the director knows the individual's problems and aspirations, his external circumstances and his talents, and the way the Holy Spirit operates in his soul.

This personal direction consists, as the definition states, in "instruction and encouragement." In themselves these two words are hardly adequate to express all the functions of the spiritual director, but they do indicate the two principal ways in which, according to circumstances, he is to exert his influence on his charge: namely, on the *intellect* by instruction, and on the *will* and the *emotions* by encouragement.

As for his influence on the intellect, the director's

work may vary from the active function of telling the individual what to do and how to do it to the almost passive function of simply approving or disapproving the plans made by the individual. He gives pointed moral and ascetical advice, he answers questions, and he corrects erroneous notions. As regards the will and the emotions, the director not only encourages, but he consoles in time of sorrow, strengthens in time of weakness, tranquilizes in time of distress, and restrains in time of imprudent ardor. In all these functions, the director must have regard for what he judges to be the designs of God on the soul of the individual committed to his care.

Some individual direction seems a practical necessity for the average religious to make safe and constant progress in perfection. This is a general rule that admits of exceptions. God can accomplish wonders in the soul directly, but most often He uses the human means of direction.

Although, according to the general rule, all religious require some individual direction, the degree and the kind of help they need, as well as the frequency with which they need it, may vary greatly. This relativity can be readily understood by referring to the twofold function of the director. Young religious, particularly novices, are likely to need a great deal of intellectual help. They are unaccustomed to self-study, to making appropriate resolutions, choosing useful subjects for the particular examen, and so forth; and they need guidance in these matters lest they waste much time and effort. To them, ascetical principles are still merely theoretical, and they often need help to see how these principles apply practically to their own lives.

But dependence on a director for intellectual help should certainly decrease with the years. Religious who have finished their training and taken their final vows should be able to plan for themselves; and their need of the spiritual director, insofar as intellectual help is concerned, should be mainly for friendly criticism. In other words, these religious plan their own lives, submit their plan to a director for approval, and then occasionally make a report on the success or failure of the plan. Naturally, one must make allowance, even with mature religious, for occasions when they face new problems or undergo special difficulties. They may need very detailed guidance at such times.

As regards the need of the director's help for the will and the emotions, it is perhaps impossible to formulate any general rule. True, to a great extent progress in the religious life should develop emotional stability. Nevertheless, neither physical age nor emotional growth frees us entirely from such trials as discouragement, loneliness, and worry; indeed, advancing age often accentuates such problems. At various periods in our lives most of us need sympathetic help or paternal correction lest we lose heart or lower our ideals.

The ordinary sources of spiritual direction for religious are their own superiors and those appointed as their confessors or spiritual directors. It seems to me that the notion of spiritual direction by the superior needs special emphasis because one reaction to the Church's ruling against obligatory manifestation of conscience has been a swing to the opposite extreme, namely, that superiors are too rarely consulted even in matters in which they are both qualified and willing to give advice. Either extreme is an evil. The present ecclesiastical legislation safeguards what is of prime importance, the perfect liberty of the individual conscience; but, granted this liberty, much good can come to the superior, the subject and to the family spirit of a community, from voluntary manifestation of conscience. Hence, the same canon which forbids religious superiors to induce their subjects to make a manifestation of conscience contains this added provision: "Subjects, however, are not forbidden to open their minds freely and spontaneously to their superiors; nay more, it is desirable that they approach their superiors with filial confidence, and, if the superiors be priests, expose to them their doubts and troubles of conscience also." Thus the Church unreservedly praises voluntary manifestation to priest superiors. As for lay superiors, there is some reservation about encouraging the manifestation of doubts and troubles of conscience, but this should not be interpreted as a prohibition.

The preceding paragraphs concern personal direction—that is, the direction of one individual by another. This is certainly what we ordinarily and primarily mean by spiritual direction. Yet, the expression is not limited to such personal relationships; it can also include more general things, such as the rules of a religious institute, books about ascetical practices, spiritual conferences, and so forth. After all, these matters, though not in themselves individualized, do provide instruction and encouragement for those who seek perfection. Sometimes they are the only sources available.

I can now return to my initial statement: that the first three sections of this book are intended as helps in the spiritual direction of religious. I believe that directors themselves may find much in these sections that they can make their own and adapt to the individuals whom they direct; and I hope that, by using these various topics as spiritual reading, individual religious may apply them to themselves and thus obtain helpful guidance. The fourth section contains material that should be useful to religious who must give spiritual direction to the laity—to students, for example. Thus, the first three sections are intended primarily for the guidance *of* religious, whereas the main purpose of the last section is guidance *by* religious. It will readily be seen, however, that this disjunction is not perfect, because many of the points in the last section should be helpful to religious themselves and much of the material in the other sections can be of profit in the guidance of the laity.

Almost all of this material has been published in the pages of *Review for Religious,* and some of it has already been made available on a rather wide scale in the form of reprints. Nevertheless, according to many retreat masters and spiritual directors, this book is both useful and needed because it brings together into a single volume a number of essays that they have found very helpful and that they wish to use frequently.

[xi]

PART $\boxed{\text{I}}$

Emotional Adjustments in Religion

Life implies not only physical but also psychological growth. This psychological growth is usually achieved by means of continuous emotional adjustments. The basic notions underlying sound emotional adjustment are common to all walks of life, but the particular situations in which the adjustments must be made will obviously differ according to the various states of life. In the first chapter of this section, I have tried to state these basic notions by outlining the characteristics of emotional maturity, and also to indicate in a general way their various applications to the religious life as a whole.

However, for the young religious there are two adjustments which, I believe, are worthy of special consideration. The first concerns the transition from one's blood family to the religious family. The second concerns the central sacrifice that characterizes the state of virginity: the renunciation of the specific

[1]

*joys and privileges that pertain to the legitimate satis-
faction of the sexual instinct. In the chapter on family
spirit, I have dealt with the first of these adjustments;
in the chapter on the particular friendship, I have
considered one aspect of the sexual renunciation required of religious. I say "one aspect," because it is
obvious that the sexual instinct operates on two
planes, the psychological and the physical, and I have
limited my treatment to the former. This is not to
imply that a treatment of the physical aspect of sex
is not important or not needed. It is very important
and much needed; but I confess that I have never
had time to write it, and the best I can do is refer
novice masters and mistresses to the suggestions in-
corporated into the chapter on emotional maturity.*

*Although these three chapters do not cover all the
special adjustments that must be made in religion,
they do treat some of the main problems and give at
least a general notion of the others. I can say quite
frankly that I gathered much of this material for my
own personal use and have found it helpful. And as
I know that many others have found it helpful, too,
I trust that those who use this book will have a similar experience.*

chapter 1

Emotional Maturity

PSYCHOLOGISTS seem to agree that one of the principal causes of failure to make the adjustments required in married life is emotional immaturity on the part of husband, or wife, or both. An expert marriage counselor is expected to give each prospective bride and groom at least some simple, but effective, maturity test; and, if he finds any notable deficiency from the accepted standard of emotional adulthood, he is to warn his client that until the defect is remedied marriage would be inadvisable. Similarly, when called upon to give advice concerning a marriage that is already being strained by maladjustments, one of the first things an expert counselor looks for is the personality defect of immaturity.

The present chapter is based on the supposition that emotional maturity is required in the religious life no less than in marriage, and that immaturity explains many of the failures to make necessary adjustments to the demands of the religious life, just as it explains similar failures in marriage. If this is true —and I have no doubt that it is—then we can profitably avail ourselves of the psychologists' excellent studies on maturity in examining candidates for the religious life, in the guidance of other religious, and in the self-examination and self-reformation necessary for our own growth in perfection.

It is with the last point that I am particularly concerned now. I believe that even professed religious can gain much for their own souls, much help in developing a Christlike personality, by studying and applying to themselves what the psychologists say about emotional maturity. The ordinary examinations of conscience tend to become dull; and many of the expressions used fail to grip the mind and to provide the proper incentive for improvement. New light and new inspiration can be infused into these self-examinations by occasionally, at least, going over a list of questions developing this one theme: "Am I the adult I should be, or am I, despite my years in religion, still childish in some things?"

The word "childish" is used designedly. Our Lord Himself has told us we must all become as little children in order to gain the kingdom of heaven; hence there is a sense in which the truly spiritual man must always be a child. On the other hand, St. Paul warns us we must grow up and put aside the things of a child. Since there can be no conflict between the words of Christ and the inspired words of Paul, I take it that these two meanings are perfectly harmonized by distinguishing between "childlikeness" and "childishness." Even one who is fully grown in Christ must be childlike; he must possess the simplicity, the candor, the humility, the sweet trust in God that come so naturally to the child. But the adult should not be childish.

[4]

What is this childishness that conflicts with true adulthood? I can best explain it, I think, by a running survey of signs of emotional immaturity culled from a number of psychological treatises. For instance, here are the test questions of immaturity that struck me as occurring most frequently: Do you indulge in angry outbursts, nurse grudges, dwell on what you consider injustices? Are you hesitant in making decisions? Do you dodge responsibility? Do you explain failures by giving alibis? Are you unable to face reality? Do you act mainly for personal pleasure and for some immediate good? Are you unable to make reasonable compromises, unwilling to make an effort to see the point of view of those who disagree with you? Are you one who wants much but gives little? Do you think you are always misunderstood, yet never misunderstand others? Do you react vehemently, even explosively, to ordinary emotional stimuli? Are you overly dependent on others, much given to fear, and to daydreaming? Do you shrink from and avoid self-sacrifice? Are you impatient of distressing situations?

Though but a partial list, this is enough to make a serious-minded religious catch his breath, for very likely most of us can find something of ourselves in the distressing portrait. Fortunately, the psychologists themselves add a consoling word: they allow for occasional lapses into some of these faults even for the mature personality. In fact, some of them use a system of grading which might well supplant numbers in the marking of a particular examen. They list faults such as these (or the opposite positive qualities) and ask the client to grade himself according to this scale: (a) never, (b) occasionally, (c) as often as not, (d) more often than not, (e) always—or almost always. Any of the faults listed in the previous paragraph that occurred with a relative frequency (for example, as often as not) would indicate the personality defect of immaturity.

It helps to examine ourselves occasionally and to see whether we possess any of these marks of childishness. Really to face the fact that a certain habit is childish is a step towards correcting it, for no one wants to be, or to be considered, childish. However, I do not wish to delay here on the negative side of the picture; I prefer to dwell on the characteristics of maturity.

Just what is emotional maturity? In general, it means the attainment of "sweet reasonableness"; it means a well-integrated personality; it means the possession of certain qualities that enable one to preserve peace within himself and to live and work harmoniously with others. I would not pretend to give a definitive list of these qualities; but from my reading and personal observation I should say that they can be fairly well summed up as follows: (a) decisive thinking, (b) unselfishness, (c) a sense of personal responsibility for the common good, (d) temperate emotional reactions, (e) a well-balanced attitude regarding sex, (f) ability to profit by criticism, and (g) ability to face reality.

It is practically impossible to comment fully on any one of these characteristics to the exclusion of the others, because a person could hardly possess one of them without possessing some of the others. Nevertheless, we can at least try to consider them singly, with special emphasis on points that seem to be of most value to religious.

Decisive Thinking

What do the psychologists mean by decisive thinking? It seems that a person who possesses this quality could be described somewhat as follows: "He is able to make calm and reasonable practical judgments, without wasting time in making them, and without feeling disturbing regret or shifting the responsibility once they are made."

A practical judgment concerns action; it is a decision concerning something to be done: for example, to clean one's desk, to practice a certain mortification. It includes such trifling things as deciding what shoes to wear and such important ones as choosing a vocation. Life is full of things to be done, and it is obvious that an adult must possess a certain facility in deciding such matters for himself according to sound principles. He must not be overly dependent on others or waste time deciding trifles, but must make his decisions, even the smallest, according to some reasonable standard. All this, and more, I have tried to compress into this brief description of mature thinking.

The ability to make a *reasonable* decision supposes the ability to make *some* decision. There are people who never make a decision for themselves if they can avoid it. When faced with a practical decision, they immediately think of seeking advice, of getting someone else to make the decision for them. Left to themselves, they flounder helplessly, unable to choose between two possible courses of action, even when mere trifles are concerned. This indecisiveness can become a pathological condition known as *abulia* (inability to make up one's own mind).

In this connection I remember an incident that happened several years ago. A friend of mine came to me and declared somewhat mournfully:

"You know, I think I'm getting abulia."

"Why," I asked, "what's wrong with you?"

"Well," he replied, "I just stood in the center of my room for half an hour trying to make up my mind whether I'd sweep it."

The example may sound, and is, absurd; yet I wonder how many of us could say that we have so trained ourselves to decide trifles that we never lose time, nor peace of mind, in making such decisions. Whether to sweep one's room, to make one's bed, to pay a visit to the Blessed Sacrament, to do without butter for one meal, to study this or that—these are examples of the countless small things a mature person should be able to decide promptly, without losing time and without seeking advice.

The psychologists do not intend to frown upon all asking of advice. The prudent man seeks counsel, but not in everything—only in matters of some moment, or when there is a special reason for mental confusion. And even in things of moment the prudent man will try to form some judgment of his own; he will not leave all the thinking to his counselors.

The childish fault of excessive advice-seeking is in-

dulged in not merely by those who will form no judgment of their own, but also by others who do indeed
form a judgment of their own (in fact, a very obsti-
nate judgment) and yet feel within themselves a certain insecurity. These advice-for-security-seekers, having made up their own minds, frequently consult
many others—but all to one purpose: namely, to get
confirmation of the plan already settled on.

The mere fact that one can make up one's own
mind promptly and, to a certain degree, independently is not in itself a sign of maturity. Indeed, this
can be very childish, unless the decision is a reasonable one—based on sound principle, in other words,
and not on mere feelings or impulses. Every mature
decision, even the tiniest, even one made with the utmost dispatch, should upon analysis reveal the fact
that a choice was made according to sound motivation, with an appreciation of the values of the course
chosen and of the course rejected.

On this point, as usual, Catholic asceticism is in
perfect agreement with the soundest psychology. For
instance, the purpose of Saint Ignatius' *Spiritual Exercises* is, in his own words, to enable one to come to
a decision without being influenced by inordinate attachments. The exercises themselves are very long
and, made in their entirety, take approximately thirty
days; but it should not be forgotten that they were
planned primarily to help one choose one's vocation.
This is a momentous decision, and it should consume
much time. The lesson of the exercises once learned,
however, is supposed to be applied all through life in
due proportion, so that every practical decision

should be made on principle and independently of excessive likes and dislikes. The underlying principle is the same for small things and for great things —God's will. To make all one's choices according to that standard is to be Christlike, is to be a saint, is to be perfectly mature.

Examining one for mature judgment, the psychologist is almost sure to ask: "When you make a decision, do you rest in it, or do you keep going over it in your mind, regretting it, wondering whether it shouldn't have been otherwise, wondering whether you shouldn't reconsider it, and so forth?" He is not implying that it is not the part of a prudent and mature person to change a decision when circumstances indicate that a change should be made. He is referring rather to an attitude of unrest, of regret, of insecurity, of changeableness, that seems to characterize almost all the practical decisions some people make.

We see this at times in young religious (and occasionally in some not so young) in the matter of their vocation. Today they feel fine and have a vocation; tomorrow they have the blues and no vocation. One wonders whether they really chose their vocation on principle. Was it the will of God or their own feelings that they chose to follow? I would not pretend to explain all the reasons for this spirit of unrest that accompanies many practical decisions; however, one reason may be that the original choice was never made wholeheartedly, with a clear appreciation of the values involved, and, consequently, the unrest comes from the fact that one is constantly wondering whether the decision was worth making. I might illustrate this by referring to a very significant picture I once noticed in a vocational booklet. In the picture are two girls, one holding a hat, the other holding five dollars; and the caption reads: "Five dollars or the hat!" The lesson doesn't have to be explained; any girl who reads the booklet can immediately catch the application: if she wants the hat badly enough, she will pay the five dollars—and if she wants the advantages of a religious vocation badly enough, she will pay the price. But the price has to be paid; she cannot have the advantages of both the religious life and life in the world any more than she can have both the hat and the price of the hat.

The appreciation of this notion of relative values is essential to all really mature thinking—and for all intelligent practice of virtue in the religious life. The decision to sweep one's room should be based on the appreciation of the advantages (natural and supernatural) that are attached to this action, as well as on the appreciation of the fact that making this precise choice involves a wholehearted "giving up" of the advantages (whatever they may be) of not sweeping the room. A choice made thus is reasonable, and it should not take half an hour. Similarly—but on a higher plane—a resolution to practice a certain mortification or to exercise oneself in a certain virtue ought to be made with a realization of the benefits one hopes to gain as well as of certain other advantages one has to reject. This idea of value for value, of paying the price, should be clearly applied in every decision, and should be resolutely recalled when one tends to weaken in following out such a decision.

This may be a sort of doubling on my tracks, but

I should like to mention here a book that once created quite a commotion in this country. I am referring to *Their Mothers' Sons* by Doctor Edward Strecker, a Catholic psychiatrist who had extensive experience screening young men drafted for the armed forces. This experience convinced him that a large percentage of our young men are afflicted with an emotional disease called "momism." In other words, despite physical maturity, they are still tied to their mothers' apron strings; their mother—or someone else—has not allowed them to grow up, to live their own lives with any real independence. Exaggerated dependence on their parents has made it impossible for them really to leave home and to stand on their own feet. This is one reason why large numbers of men failed in the acid test of military service, one reason why many marriages fail. One may well wonder just what influence it has on religious.

It is not inconceivable that young men and women may enter religion without having accomplished any real separation from the parental apron strings. It is possible, too, that this exaggerated dependence on parents may spoil an otherwise promising vocation, or that the ingrained dependence may merely be transferred from parents to a kindly superior, confessor, or spiritual director. In fact, even for those who are not unduly dependent, the religious life of its very nature contains certain dangers to proper growth in maturity. It calls for much more dependence than is normally had in adult life; and if this feature is pressed too far, it can readily change childlikeness into childishness. It is a wise superior or director or other person in authority who encourages a salutary self-confidence and a wholesome spirit of initiative in his subordinates.

Before concluding this point, I should like to refer to a notion that I recently came across in my reading. The author, speaking of a mature mind, said that it is a "hospitable mind." It welcomes new ideas; and this is the *sine qua non* of progress. And of course, being hospitable, it is also companionable. Need I say what a boon this is in a religious community?

Unselfishness

Ascetical writers say much about the need and beauty of unselfishness in their treatises on the supernatural virtue of charity. Psychologists lay an equal emphasis on the need of unselfishness for leading an adult life. By unselfishness the psychologists mean thoughtfulness of others, the ability to *give* in contradistinction to the childish tendency to *receive*. They show how men fail in business, in professional life, in social life, and above all in marriage because they think only of themselves and seek only their own gain without regard for the feelings and desires of others. They demand as a minimum for successful adult life what may be called in common parlance a "fifty-fifty" spirit, a willingness to go halfway and to give as much as one takes.

The mention of this "fifty-fifty" spirit reminds me of a very impressive remark made by a young Catholic layman at a discussion on marriage. Most of the participants in the discussion were unmarried collegians. They had almost concluded that for a successful marriage the husband and wife should both be willing to go halfway and to share burdens equally, when this young man, who had been blessedly married for several years, startled them with these words:

"I have heard and read a lot about this 'fifty-fifty' recipe for a happy marriage; but my wife and I are convinced that this isn't enough. If each is willing to go only halfway, they simply come to a dead stop. We have found that each must be willing to go more than halfway. Let's call it a 'seventy-five-seventy-five' basis; that gives fifty percent extra to run the house on."

The ideal constantly proposed to religious certainly goes beyond the psychologists' minimum standard for maturity; yet even this minimum standard is not infrequently higher than our actual practice. Selfishness is a form of childishness that is not easily laid aside. It can disguise itself in many forms and actually appear as various virtues: for example, as the necessary care of health, as the protection of one's rights, as kindness to a friend, and so forth. It can change colors like the chameleon; it can wedge into the holiest of exercises.

Even psychologists who know little of the ideals of the religious life could probably give us a very searching and illuminating examination on our unselfishness or lack of it. They have the distressing faculty of avoiding generalities and getting down to pertinent particulars. For instance, if a psychologist were allowed to invade the privacy of our examination of conscience and to question us, he would very likely include such details as these: Do you take the best food at table, or do you leave it for others? Do you try to get the newspaper first (if there is a newspaper), or do you give others this chance? Do you monopolize conversation, or show an interest in what others have to say? Do you make it a point to note what pleases others, and are you willing to do that even at the expense of your own whims?

Those are samples of the little things that show who is and who is not selfish. It is interesting to note that our rules or customs usually include such points; and for this reason we have probably come to think of them only in terms of religious perfection. It is enlightening, and perhaps humiliating, to learn that even a materialistic psychologist would examine us on those very points, not to determine whether we are saintly religious, but merely to discover whether we are really grown up.

In *Testing the Spirit,* Father Felix Duffey, C.S.C., rightly insists on the need of a wholehearted spirit of self-sacrifice in the religious life.[1] The life begins with self-oblation, and its true peace is had only by those who continue in this spirit. I have already referred to religious who show a marked indecision about their vocation because they seem never to have actually made their decision on the one sound principle—namely, the will of God. Perhaps one reason for this indecision is that such people are really seeking, not God, but self.

While I was teaching a group of sisters in summer

[1] St. Louis: B. Herder, 1947. See page 31 for Father Duffey's remarks on self-sacrifice. The second part of this book (pp. 25-98) contains a number of questions designed to help a vocational counselor to judge the emotional qualifications of a candidate for the religious life.

school, we discussed some of the characteristics of emotional maturity. The class agreed that in actual life some of the marks of the truly unselfish person would be a tolerant attitude, courtesy, tact, a ready spirit of cooperation, and consideration for the feelings and moods of others.

One thing that all of us should keep in mind is this: a religious gives up the normal consolations of family life, yet it is doubtful whether anyone can entirely divest himself of the fundamental craving for love and attention. Some people do this exteriorly; but usually they suffer much interiorly over it, or the repression does some damage to their personality. Part of the supreme art of living the religious life is to show others the kindness and sympathy for which they naturally crave without letting one's charity degenerate into sensuous or particular friendships. Each religious community is a family, and the members should be bound together by an affection that is familial. The unselfish person realizes this and is warm and approachable without being soft and sentimental.

Community Responsibility

In speaking of unselfishness, I was thinking primarily in terms of thoughtfulness of others *as individuals.* This is a beautiful character trait, but it is not enough for maturity. The mature person must also be group conscious, that is, alive to his responsibility to promote the common good. This subject offers religious a vast field for personal examination; for our lives are of necessity *community lives,* and

[16]

the success or failure of the whole venture depends on the cooperation of each individual. No one can do it all; anyone can spoil it all—at least in some sense.

How can we test ourselves with regard to this sense of personal responsibility in common enterprises? The psychologist, I believe, would examine us on all the community aspects of our lives. He would very likely ask about such small points as this: Do you turn off radiators and lights when they are not needed? And he would put questions of greater moment, such as: Do you help to keep certain privileges like the radio, movies, and victrola by not abusing them? And he would want to know especially about your public conduct; for example: Do you speak well of your community? Do you act always in such a way that you give no one grounds for thinking ill of your community, your institute, the religious life, the whole Church?

That would be a general formula for the psychologist's questions: the little things, the things of greater moment, the things of tremendous import. Into this general scheme he would insert many other questions besides those I mentioned—for instance: Do you observe library rules so that all have a chance to read the books? Do you enter into special community projects, like helping the missions? When you play games, are you content to work for the team or do you want the spotlight even at the expense of the team?

Very likely we could list pages of pertinent questions, but there is no need of doing that here. Each one who wishes to examine himself on this aspect of maturity can formulate his own questions. The essential point behind all such questions is to determine whether the religious *realizes* that he is a part of a community and that all the interests of that community are his interests. He works with the community at home; he represents the community to outsiders. His lack of cooperation at home can spoil the harmony of common life and dull the effectiveness of the community as an apostolic instrument; his disloyalty or bad example before outsiders can literally bring about a spiritual catastrophe.

Superiors can do much to foster the sense of community responsibility in their subjects, especially by keeping them well-informed about community affairs and projects. Some superiors seem to think that they are the official worriers for the community and they tell their communities little or nothing about business plans and such things. Everything is a solemn secret, even the name of the next retreat director. It is true, of course, that some things must be kept secret; but exaggerated secretiveness is hardly calculated to foster a personal community interest in the individual members. When treated as children, they are quite apt to react as children.

Temperate Emotional Reactions

Emotions are a part of human life. Granted an appropriate stimulus, there ought to be some spontaneous emotional reaction: for instance, the sight of sorrow should provoke sympathy; the perception of kindness should prompt gratitude; the consciousness of imminent danger should stimulate fear. Such reactions are normal. Some men seem to have such dominating control over their emotions that they either do not react to normal stimuli or they repress the reaction so swiftly that it is perceptible to none save themselves. This is not necessarily virtue, not necessarily true maturity; on the contrary, it may be quite inhuman. The "poker face" is neither a psychological nor an ascetical ideal. Our Lord certainly showed emotional reactions—fear, pity, joy, and the like—although He was capable, if He so wished, of suppressing even the slightest reaction.

True maturity, therefore, consists in responding properly and temperately to emotional stimuli. To show no emotion is inhuman; to react with undue vehemence is immature. Calm anger may be justified both morally and psychologically; a wild outburst is never the proper reaction. Hearty laughter may be the adult reaction to a humorous situation or anecdote, but hysterical giggling and wild guffaws are signs of immaturity. Both adult and child may feel fear, and both may and should run away from danger when there is no reason for facing it; but when duty calls, the true adult will control his fear and face the danger.

Psychologically, the specific difference between adult and childish emotional reactions lies in *control*. The adult reaction is held to moderation; the childish response is an explosive outburst. The problem of maturity is to acquire such control of the emotions that undesirable ones are eliminated or calmly suppressed as much as possible and desirable ones are used with moderation. For example, although the kind of love that leads to marriage is good in itself, it is undesirable for religious; hence, situations that would foster it should be quietly avoided. On the other hand, a tender love of God, provided it has real spiritual substance, is desirable and is to be cultivated. And so it is with many other emotions: sorrow for sin, sympathy with our Lord, affection for our friends—all such things can help greatly in the religious life; and the mature attitude towards them should be one of reasonable use.

As I suggested previously, it is easy to cull the literature of psychology for questions to bring out the negative side of any matter, and this is particularly true of emotional control. For example, here are some of the negatives: Do you easily become fretful? Are you impatient to carry out your impulses? Do you explode over a tiny offense? Are you a victim of moods—up today and down tomorrow? Do you nurse injured feelings for a long time? Are you frequently disturbed by haunting fears? Do you indulge in serious weeping spells? Do you "sulk in your tent"? Do you look upon yourself as a martyr or the victim of misunderstanding and injustice? Do you easily grow hilarious?

The purpose of these and similar questions is clear. If reactions such as those just mentioned are *characteristic* of a person, he is immature. On the other hand, if he usually manifests poise, if he readily adjusts himself interiorly to emotionally stimulating situations—he is an adult.

We can conclude this section by quoting a de-

scription of adult emotional control given by Father
Raphael McCarthy, S.J.:

> The management of one's emotions demands vari-
> ous kinds of repressions. It means that a man responds
> with the emotion that is justified by the circumstances;
> he does not allow himself to become passionate over
> minor provocations and he ceases to be excited when
> the cause of his emotion is passed. Self-government im-
> plies, also, that a man can moderate his affective reac-
> tions; he can make partial responses, so that he can
> feel fear without being thrown into panic, he is not
> swept into a towering rage by trifling oppositions, nor
> does he bellow when his hat is blown off by the wind.
> He can, moreover, check the physical expression of his
> emotion so that he does not strike out like an imbecile
> when he is angered, or dash away like a terrified child
> when he is frightened.[2]

Attitude on Sex

There is, at least in many instances, a rather close
connection between one's general emotional control
and one's attitude on sex. This will be clear, I think,
if we consider briefly what should be the mature
attitude on sex.

The adult should be well-informed about the purpose of sex and the meaning of chastity. Not that he
needs to know everything about sex, for there are
some aspects of sex that are definitely pathological
and that need be known only by experts. But an
adult should know the normal phenomena pertaining to the psychology and physiology of sex, and the
moral and ascetical principles that apply to the sex-

2 *Safeguarding Mental Health* (Milwaukee: Bruce, 1937), p. 287.

ual sphere. Without such correct knowledge he is liable to experience the adolescent's embarrassment in the presence of others, as well as a curiosity that easily becomes morbid. Moreover, without such knowledge, he is unable to make a correct estimate of his own reactions to persons and situations, and this may lead to regrettable imprudences, to extreme sensitivity, and to scrupulosity. He comes to fear sin everywhere because he really does not know what sin is, and he cannot cope quietly with temptation because he does not know clearly what is expected of him. Ignorance and anxiety in a matter so fundamental and important as sex are almost certain to have an unwholesome effect on one's personality and to hinder the full development of the other characteristics of maturity.

It goes without saying that those who are to take a vow of chastity should have a clear understanding of the meaning of this vow; and it is the duty of the novice master or mistress to see that they get it. As a matter of fact, explaining the duties of the vow of chastity entails no special difficulties for those who already know the duties imposed by the virtue of chastity on all unmarried people, because the vow simply confirms these duties and adds the obligation of refraining from marriage. Consequently, novice masters and mistresses should themselves have a clear knowledge of the moral principles pertinent to chastity outside of marriage and should be able to impart these to others. It is taken for granted that a priest novice master has this qualification. Brothers and sisters who are entrusted with the guidance of novices should acquire the necessary knowledge either by private study or, preferably, by attending one of the courses now offered in many of our schools that include this particular matter.[3]

In general, the goal for religious, as regards chastity, is to be able to lead the life of virginity with interior peace and exterior graciousness. To do this, one must have a fine combination of idealism and common sense. The idealism should be based on sound principles. This implies not only a speculative knowledge of the pertinent physical and psychological aspects of sex, as well as the moral and ascetical principles, but also an interior appreciation of the beauty of virginity and a consequent genuine desire to practice it perfectly. It must be admitted that a not uncommon source of mental disquiet among religious is the fact that they develop the habit of "playing close to the line," of taking "little chances" in their reading, their entertainment, and similar matters. True idealism rejects such halfheartedness and, in so doing, it is not only morally and ascetically correct but also psychologically wholesome.

But idealism must be tempered by common sense. Common sense helps us to realize that what is involuntary cannot be sinful and that we simply do not have perfect control over our thoughts, phantasms, and feelings. Thoughts may be very persistent, phan-

[3] Both masters and mistresses of novices may profit by reading *Modern Youth and Chastity* (St. Louis: Queen's Work, 1943), which contains a thorough general treatment of chastity and the sex instinct. Novice mistresses can obtain additional help from the *Proceedings* of the 1953 and 1954 Sisters' Institutes of Spirituality (Notre Dame, Ind.: University of Notre Dame Press).

tasms may be very vivid, and feelings may be very strong, yet the person with common sense can preserve interior peace because he knows that he neither seeks nor wills to have these things. Common sense also reminds us that external sources of temptation cannot be entirely avoided. We cannot go through life, as it were, with dark glasses; certainly in our present world we cannot avoid many things that disturb the imagination or stimulate the emotions. On the other hand, common sense (as well as idealism) does prompt us to avoid these sources of temptation as much as is reasonably possible when they are not connected with other things that are either necessary or useful.

Emotionally mature religious should be able to deal with the other sex with friendliness and reserve. Thus, they need not deny the existence of the natural attraction, but they must keep it properly controlled. Incidentally, it is not a sign of maturity to be a "man-hater" or a "woman-hater." This attitude is not normal. Sometimes it has been developed consciously, because of some morbid past experience; and sometimes it is merely a mask for one's real feelings.

Profiting by Criticism

"Are you sincerely grateful to those who point out your faults to you?" I was more than a little startled when I read that question in a maturity test drawn up by a man who, I feel sure, has little knowledge of Catholic asceticism. He was thinking only in terms of sound psychology; yet he included in his test a quality which we tend to look for only in the saints. Let us consider this in terms of our own experience in the religious life. Spiritual directors often tell religious that they should be *patient* when others point out their faults; in fact, it is generally said that religious should be *willing* to have their faults pointed out by others; and at times the directors do speak of gratitude. But my impression is that, when there is question of religious of only ordinary virtue, their directors tell them to be grateful *to God*. They scarcely dare to counsel gratitude *to the critic*; rather, they seem content with hoping that criticism will not be the occasion of angry outbursts or of long-continued grudges. But the psychologist unhesitatingly demands gratitude to the critic; the psychologist dares to enter where the spiritual director fears to tread.

Perhaps I have underestimated the virtue of religious and have made the picture too black. Yet, if superiors, spiritual directors, and critics could all pool their experiences and thus determine the average reaction of religious when corrected, I wonder what the result would be. Would it be that correction is the cause of an angry outburst, of sullen silence, of tears over the "evident injustice," or of a defiant mind-your-own-business attitude? Would it be that correction is generally answered with a "Why don't you say something to the other fellow"? Or would it be that correction is usually received with quiet resignation, with depressed spirits but an honest attempt to be grateful to God "for the humiliation," or with a certain eagerness to know the truth and with gratitude towards the one who had the courage to point it out?

Some moral theologians use an expression that is

in remarkable agreement with the question put by the psychologist. They refer to fraternal correction as a "spiritual almsgiving." The implication, of course, is that the critic is doing one a favor and is therefore deserving of thanks. And obviously anyone who realizes that it is really good for him to know his faults should be grateful to the person who helps him in this regard. Hence, it seems that what the psychologists call maturity in this matter is actually the ability to appreciate true values: one realizes the utility of knowing one's own faults and the difficulty usually experienced by those who have to point them out.

Are we, therefore, childish when we resent criticism? It seems that usually we are. Yet there are some special factors that may make a difference. For instance, some offer criticism in an offensive manner; others offer it through spite and without sincerity; and of course there are those people who have so cultivated the art of fault-finding that they see faults where there are none. Even in cases like these the adult should receive criticism with composure, but there seems to be little need for gratitude.

While I am on the subject of profiting by criticism, I might mention that an adult, even when grateful to his critic, should receive the criticism intelligently. Whether it be a criticism of one's character, of one's writings, or of anything else, it should be weighed carefully before it is followed.

Facing Reality

Reality is life, the whole of life; but when psychologists speak of facing reality, they seem to be thinking particularly in terms of one's capacity for attempting what is difficult and for adjusting oneself to painful situations. Speaking of men who shrink from reality or are broken by reality, they give such examples as these: patients who enjoy the hospital because it affords them loving attention and dependence and shelters them from the burdens of work and responsibility; workers who go along nicely in a subordinate position but break when they receive a promotion; men who can live a quiet life but break when they must be active; persons who thrive on activity but cannot stand the monotony of a quiet life; men who overindulge in recreation or avoid the realities of life by taking to alcohol; the wife who runs to her mother at the first sign of trouble or responsibility in marriage.

Little test questions sometimes used to determine whether one has the adult ability to face reality might run somewhat like this: When you are given a job that you are afraid of or dislike, do you try to get out of it either openly or by excuses that you know are not valid? Do you get upset or go to pieces when faced with a new situation that will force you out of a rut? Are you given to daydreaming? When you fail, do you justify yourself by a lame excuse or do you admit the failure and try again? Do you find that you are wasting more and more time, finding many useless things to do, before you settle down to the real work of the day? Do you dread responsibility and try to evade it? Do you neglect the present by thinking and talking in terms of your glorious past or by boasting of your glorious future?

For us religious, reality is to a great extent the

duty of the moment. Disagreeable or not, that duty is God's will—and that is the supreme test of reality. Still, we do have an amazing power of dodging, consciously or unconsciously, the disagreeable tasks. One religious neglects his studies to engage, as he says, in "works of the apostolate." Another accomplishes the same result with equal ingenuity by deciding that "he has no head for books," but he can fit himself for his future work by playing games or making gadgets. And still another shirks the monotony of prayer and study with the consoling observation that he was "cut out for the active life."

Failure and disappointment are among the hard realities of life. The adult is expected to face them with composure when they threaten and to adjust himself quietly to them when they occur. Yet is it not true that all too many religious have been broken and soured by such things? Do we not see, at least occasionally, a religious who, though still comparatively young, is useless for further work in the cause of Christ because he has been denied the fulfillment of some ambition?

Here is a problem that I believe is not uncommon among us. As we move on through our years of training we note a great desire for accomplishment, yet on the other hand a great fear to undertake the very things we so much desire. We feel a dread of responsibility, which, if fostered, can ruin our whole lives. I know of one sound defense against this: namely, to make up one's mind to try anything that is assigned by superiors and never to try to avoid it unless there is some really good reason for asking the superior to reconsider the matter. A religious who begins to yield to such fears may soon find that his self-confidence is utterly destroyed.

We can conclude this point by referring for a moment to the life of our Lord. From the first moment of His life He was conscious of two tremendous future events: the Cross and the Resurrection; and the actual living of His life—as far as the records show—presents a similar pattern: failure and success, pain and joy, the bitter and the sweet. In His life, too, were the security of obeying and the responsibility of commanding, the doing of little things and the accomplishing of great things, the quiet hidden life and the bustling active life. It is a complex pattern; yet through it runs a wondrously simplifying theme— it was all His Father's will. The same pattern runs through our lives, and the best tonic for fear and disappointment is the abiding consciousness of God's loving providence. One who has this consciousness, who is able to see the hand of God and the plan of God in all the events of his life, is scarcely in danger of becoming emotionally unstable; he is admirably mature.

chapter 2

Family Spirit

It is traditional usage in the Church to refer to a religious institute or community as "a religious family." This expression is rich in meaning, and all of us can profit by occasionally reflecting on it. The present chapter is designed to provide a stimulus for such reflections; it is by no means calculated to do full justice to the possibilities.

Leaving the Old

In itself, the expression "a religious family" has a positive meaning. It signifies that the religious community is a family in its own right with the duties and privileges that belong to real family life. But this positive element presupposes something negative: a break with one's natural family. Without separation from the old there can never be complete incorporation into the new. Logically, therefore, our reflections ought first to be directed towards this negative element, separation.

It is well to note at the outset that separation from parents and relatives is not easy. It is very difficult indeed. Nevertheless, it would be a mistake for religious to think that only they are called upon to make this sacrifice. As a matter of fact, even children who marry must effect the same separation if their married life is to be a success. All the best psychological studies of failures in marriage stress that one of the principal causes of trouble is the fact that one or both parties remain "tied to their mother's apron strings." The truth of this research merely illustrates the inspired words of Genesis (2:24): "Wherefore, a man shall leave father and mother and shall cleave to his wife." Married people must realize that they are starting a new family and that they must break definitely with the old. The same is true of religious.

In this matter of separation we have both the example and the words of our Lord to show us the way. When He was twelve, He permitted the hearts of those He loved most dearly to be filled with anguish because He must be about His Father's business. Years later He parted definitely with the finest of mothers and the best of companions in order to give Himself to three tireless years of His Father's business and to climax it all with His crucifixion. And He confirmed this example by strong words about the need of separation. In Matthew (10:37) we read: "He that loveth father or mother more than me is not worthy of me"; and in Luke (14:26) the even stronger words: "If any man come to me and hate not his father and mother and wife and children and brethren and sisters, yea and his own life also, he cannot be my disciple."

It is obvious that, despite the force of His words, our Lord is not telling us that we must tear the love of parents and relatives out of our hearts. His own love for His Mother was deep, intense, and tender, and it remained so all His life. Yet it would have been an imperfect thing, and unworthy of Him, had it urged Him to stay with her one moment longer than the divine plan permitted, or had it been allowed in any way to interfere with His apostolate. This is the model of our own affection for parents and relatives. We are supposed to love them; we are bound to them by ties of blood and gratitude. But that love must be well ordered. It must not interfere, even slightly, with the purpose of our religious life, for to achieve that purpose is our Father's business.

From the beginning of our religious life we have to set ourselves resolutely to accomplish the physical and mental separation from parents and relatives that allows us to give ourselves quietly and wholeheartedly to our religious duties. And one of the first and most important lessons we must learn is to entrust our dear ones to divine providence. It often happens that a religious has hardly entered the novitiate when he begins to receive distressing news from home: Father has lost his job, Mother needs a serious operation, a baby niece has diphtheria, a nephew was in a terrible accident, the black sheep of the family has got into some new trouble. News of this kind will be more or less frequent all through our religious lives. Unless we adjust ourselves properly to it, it can be the source of constant anxiety that spoils our mental prayer, diminishes the efficiency of our work, and even tempts us to abandon our vocation. Of course, it isn't easy to rid ourselves of such anxiety. We cannot just say, "I won't be anxious," and thus put all the worrisome thoughts to rout. But in a positive way we can cultivate the attitude that in leaving parents and relatives we are putting them into the hands of God and that, if we give our thoughts to God and our own vocation, God will take care of our dear ones. After all, we are not the only ones who need a great trust in divine providence.

Letter writing is another test of well-ordered love of parents and relatives. It is one thing for a young religious to write home every day and another to write so seldom that parents can justly complain of neglect. It is one thing to write pages and pages of small talk and another to write, "Dear Mom: I'm fine; hope you're the same. Love." These examples are extreme, but not entirely fictional. It is well for religious to cultivate the habit of writing home at regular intervals and to keep that habit as long as their parents are living. The letters need not be long, but they should not be too short, either. A letter is neither a book nor a telegram. We should try to make our letters interesting, without at the same time revealing details that should be kept within the privacy of our community or telling things that might cause needless worry. There are some mothers who, if they heard their beloved daughter had a sore knee, would immediately think in terms of an amputation. We learn through experience that innocent remarks in letters can easily assume enormous proportions. Having, as a young religious, gone to the hospital for a check-up that was little more than routine, I casually mentioned this fact in a letter to

a devoted aunt. Three weeks later my superior called
me to his room. In his hand was a telegram from the
same devoted aunt. She had just heard that her
nephew had only a short time to live and she wondered whether she should come at once. That was
the first news I had of my desperate condition. Upon
investigation, I found that my aunt had told a friend
about my check-up and, as the news passed from
friend to friend, my condition grew steadily worse.
Finally the original news, transformed by the ghastly
details of my incurability, got back to my aunt.

Then there are visits. Some time ago I presided at
a discussion group made up of mistresses of novices
and postulants of various institutes. One of the
points discussed concerned the visits to postulants and
novices by parents and relatives. The customs varied
greatly. One of the institutes simply has the absolute
custom: no visits till first vows—and this institute has
a two-year novitiate. I am not exaggerating when I
say that all the other novice- and postulant-mistresses
gasped with envy when they heard this. All agreed
that, hard though it seemed, this would be an ideal
arrangement. All complained that when visits are
allowed, the day after the visit is like beginning the
postulancy or the novitiate over again.

Some may disagree with me, but I think the religious who is stationed far from home is blessed.
This is true of monastic institutes because it prevents
too much visiting from relatives; and it is even more
true of other institutes, for it not only prevents the
visiting on the part of relatives, but it helps to preserve in the religious himself the perfect interior lib-

erty which keeps him at the free disposition of superiors. They can send him where he is most needed or most useful without fear of opposition.

Occasionally there are good reasons for being stationed near one's home, but such reasons are rather rare and are usually of short duration. Yet it is not unknown that some religious are ingenious at conjuring up reasons why they should be stationed in the shadow of their home. And sometimes the relatives themselves exert pressure to this end. These relatives have no ill will; they simply do not understand the nature of the religious life and they need to be set right on this point. The religious who wants to be a perfectly pliable instrument in the hands of God should not leave the burden of explanation to superiors. He ought himself to assume the responsibility of pointing out to his relatives that, in entering religion, he placed himself at the disposal of superiors and that he wants to work where they think he should work.

Living the New

The preceding points could be amplified and related ones added. But, since my purpose is to stress the positive aspect of our family life, I wish to devote most of my space to the elements that contribute to genuine family living in religion.

The first of these positive elements is paternal government. Someone has said that government is paternal when it manifests the "gentleness, kindliness, and love of Christ." No doubt that expresses the idea most beautifully; yet, unless we translate "paternal" into terms of ordinary family life, we shall remain in the sphere of mere theory.

A good father is supposed to be solicitous for each member of his family, while at the same time seeking the common good of the entire family. This is not easily accomplished even in a family of five or six children; it is certainly much more difficult in a religious community of ten, twenty, thirty, and even more subjects. Nevertheless the ideal is there, and it cannot be lowered without prejudice to true family life.

This ideal clearly rules out favoritism, as that word is ordinarily understood, but it hardly means that a superior cannot have any especially intimate friends within his community. It is commonly said that our Lord had a special regard for St. John; yet no one would dare accuse Him of favoritism. In the best families, parents often have a special love for one child without in any sense neglecting the others. They do not love the others less because they love him more. And we ourselves, as subjects, often have warm, intimate friendships with a few members of our community without in any way diminishing the charity we owe the others. This is human. Superiors do not (or should not) cease to be human when they take office.

Nevertheless, special friendships present a danger; and superiors, even more than others, must guard against the danger. Any superior who gives his friends privileges he would not give others, who violates confidences to satisfy their curiosity, who neglects the rest of his community to be with them, who allows them to have undue influence in the managing of the community is certainly not governing paternally.

Solicitude for the individual must always be subordinated to the interests of the group. All of us, even without having been superiors, must have experienced at times the difficulty of living up to this standard. A teacher may have a boy in his class, a thoroughly likable lad, who is constantly a drawback to the rest of the class in studies and in discipline. Or a prefect may have discovered that a youngster has been stealing or has other bad habits that are infecting the group; and he may be torn between the two unpleasant alternatives of having this boy dismissed with the probability that he will not go to another Catholic school or of keeping him in the school with risk of great harm to the others. In problems such as these the ultimate solution must be in terms of the greater good—and that is usually the common good. We should do all we can to save the individual boy, but not at the expense of the group. And the superior has to solve the similar problems that arise in community life in the same way. He will show great sympathy and tolerance for the wayward or cantankerous subject; but this tolerance has its just limit: the community has a right to its good name and to peaceful living, and its right should not be jeopardized for the individual.

A good father likes to be with his family. Every institute, I suppose, prescribes that the superior be present at community meals and community recreations and that he stay home most of the time. This is not merely for the sake of discipline; it is a requisite for good family life. I might suggest, though, that the expression "most of the time" be emphasized. A wise old Father once remarked that a good superior will make it a point to get away from his community occasionally. It is good for both the superior and the community. Absence makes the heart grow fonder. And this is also true of ordinary family life. When parents get away occasionally, both they and the children benefit by it.

When we look back on our childhood, one of the things that very likely strikes us forcibly is the memory of how our parents adjusted themselves to us. When with us, they lived in our world, the child's world; and they did not try to force us into theirs. I think this fact helps illustrate the full meaning of paternal government in religion. The good superior seeks the interests of his community; he lives in their world, not his own. For instance, he does not monopolize recreation with his own topics of conversation; or, to put the same example in another way, he does not recreate the brethren—he recreates with the brethren. Paternal government necessarily implies that the superior look upon the members of his community as his children. This is obvious; the correlative of "parent" is "child." But "child" in this context means "son or daughter"; it does not mean "infant" or even "adolescent." The paternal superior, therefore, treats his subjects as adults. He has respect for their age, their diginity, and their talents.

Many other things could be said about the paternal superior. He may be stern; he is never harsh. He fosters religious idealism by his good example. He is a good provider in accordance with the means at his disposal and the purpose of his institute. He makes sure that his subjects have plenty of time to see him. He tries to employ them according to their strength and their talents. He encourages them to develop their talents for the good of the institute and ultimately for the greater glory of God. I could go on, but I cannot develop these points without converting this into a discussion entitled "How to Be a Good Superior"—by one who has never been a superior.

The next topic concerns us, the subjects. On the basis of experience, I should know much more about this. However, it is rather human to know more about the other fellow's job. A friend of mine who was appointed a superior several years ago made a very appropriate speech on the night of his installation. "A week ago," he said, "I knew everything a superior ought to do. Tonight I'm not so sure."

In terms of the religious family, the correlative of paternal government is filial confidence. This expression is not easily explained. It seems to signify something that we recognize almost instinctively—like the taste of chocolate—yet are only faintly able to describe. A fundamental element seems to be confidence in the superior's judgment. And by this I am not referring to the fact that he is in the place of Christ: that tells me merely that I am right in obeying him, but it does not tell me that he is right in commanding. Religious life would be nothing short of a continuous miracle if all of us lived it day after day and year after year with the conviction that the superior is wrong, but we are right. For ordinary peaceful living we need the confidence that, at least generally speaking, the superiors are right, that they govern well, that their natural judgment is good. We needn't endow superiors with either infallibility or impeccability in order to gain this confidence.

If one may judge from the content of several anonymous letters sent to *Review for Religious,* some religious must think that the first requisite for becoming and remaining a superior is stupidity. The attitude of such religious is not readily diagnosed. Perhaps the cause is indigestion, or sleeplessness, or some mental maladjustment. At any rate, it is certainly pathological. And we can all thank God for that; for, if their attitude represented the normal outlook of religious subjects, we should be in a sorry state.

I am not saying there are no bad superiors, no unrealists, no martinets, no tyrants among them; but I do say most emphatically that there are enough good ones for us to preserve our confidence in the institution, even on a natural basis. And I believe that in saying this I am expressing the view of the general run of religious subjects. As a group, we have a basic confidence that our superiors govern well. This does not mean that we do not occasionally, or even frequently, think we could plan things better. Nor does it mean that we never criticize. Most of us, no doubt, indulge in enough criticism of superiors to provide matter for a periodic particular examen, for confession, and for good resolutions. We can and we should improve. Nevertheless, some criticism, provided it is not too frequent and—especially—not bitter, is no major impediment to family life.

In considering the paternal-filial relationship, reference to the manifestation of conscience is inevitable. As I have already intimated when discussing spiritual direction, the fact that the Church has forbidden superiors to demand a manifestation of conscience has been stressed to such an extent as to lead many religious to think that their conscience is simply none of the superior's business. The very nature of religious government shows this to be absurd. Superiors are supposed to assign subjects to places and offices in such a way that the individuals can save and sanctify their souls and that the general good of the institute is promoted. An assignment which defeats either of these ends defeats the purpose of the religious life itself.

Yet, how is a superior to make a wise and provident disposition of subjects according to the twofold purpose of the religious life unless he has an intimate knowledge of his subjects? And how is he to get this knowledge adequately without perfect candor on the part of the subjects? It is very saddening to hear a religious whose assignment is actually proving his spiritual ruin, say: "I just couldn't tell my superior about this difficulty." The fault may be his, or it may be his superior's; in either case, the condition is lamentable and should never have been allowed to develop. Perhaps both superiors and subjects could profit by reflecting on these words of a saintly and experienced spiritual director: "Nothing helps so effectually to engender a paternal attitude toward a subject as the account of conscience; for, when I open my heart to my superior I constrain him to take a fatherly attitude toward me and a fatherly interest in my welfare. Thereafter he cannot remain just my superior if he be a man of normal humanity. Then, this bestowal of my inmost confidence upon my superior will be powerful to effect in my soul the reciprocal relation of filial trust and love. Conversely, when I withhold my confidence from the superior and refuse to open my heart to him, I make his position difficult as far as fatherly feeling is concerned. Sometimes our superiors may seem to us to lack paternal interest. The fault may be theirs; but likewise it may be ours, due to the fact that we have never given them our confidence."

Paternal government and filial confidence are the constituent elements of family life in the superior-subject relationship. The third element is the bond of union among the members. All that we generally say concerning fraternal charity pertains to the explanation of this element. I shall content myself here with pointing out a few things that seem to have special relevance to our "family" charity.

In our mutual relationships there ought to be no quarreling, no offensive teasing, no harsh words. This certainly is the ideal of our charity, yet a wholesome family spirit can exist among us without perfection in this ideal. Consider again the analogy with the good natural family: the brothers and sisters squabble a bit, the parents lose their tempers occasionally; but they "make up fast," as the saying goes, and a short time after the explosive incidents everyone is acting as if nothing disagreeable had happened. To strive for such a mode of behavior is perhaps to have a more realistic goal in our community relationships.

Despite the noblest of resolutions, we get out of sorts and we fly off the handle. Given a group of normal human beings, these occurrences can hardly be avoided entirely in the close associations that make up community living, but we can certainly avoid prolonged teasing that hurts, continued bickering, harboring grudges, and so forth. These are things that deeply wound family spirit.

Our goal, therefore, is to love the members of our community in much the same way as the members of a good Catholic family love one another. It is hardly possible to accomplish this perfectly. There is truth in the old maxim that "blood will tell." On the purely natural plane it is often easy to preserve an intense affection for our blood brothers and sisters even when they possess characteristics that others consider unpleasant. In our dealing with others, even with fellow religious, there is much greater need of explicitly stimulating motives for love.

Certainly there are many powerful motives for mutual love among religious. One of these was expressed graphically by a military chaplain when he returned to his community after the last war: "You don't know how good it is to sit at table again with a group of men who are all in the state of grace!" These are startling words—perhaps even a bit exaggerated. Yet, isn't it true that they express a profound reason why there should be great peace in the companionship of religious? Day after day all of us say Mass or receive Holy Communion—a reasonably sure practical sign that we are living habitually in the friendship of God. There are many saintly people outside of re-

ligion, and many who, if not canonizable, do live
constantly in the state of grace; but there are many
others who are unjust, obscene, blasphemous. Even
good people in the world can scarcely avoid their
companionship, whereas in religion our lives and our
recreations are spent with companions who, despite
many small and irritating faults, are substantially
good.

Their supernatural goodness is not the only reason
why the companionship of religious should be enjoyable. Even on the natural level religious are apt to
have more likable qualities than any average group
of the laity. At least, that should be so, since we are
screened for especially undesirable qualities when
we apply for admission, as well as on the occasions of
our vows. It is true that most of us look back and
wonder how we passed the screening; and those of us
who entered before the days of intelligence and personality tests may frankly admit in the secrecy of our
hearts that, if these tests had existed in our day, we
might not have made the grade. No doubt, despite
all the screening, some serious mistakes are made;
some pass through the screening processes who later
become real menaces to community life. But the general percentage of companionable characters should
be and is much higher than it would be elsewhere.

I mentioned before that it is not uncommon for
children of the same family to fight among themselves. I have seen two small boys, brothers, literally
mauling each other over the possession of a little
wagon. Then another boy appeared and attempted to
align himself with one party. But the brothers would

have none of that! In a flash their own quarrel was ended and they were united against the intruder. This is typical of good family life. No matter how much the members fight among themselves, they present a united front to outsiders. We religious should have that spirit of family loyalty.

In some sense, at least, each of us must have looked on his own institute as the "best of all" when he entered religion; otherwise he would have joined another. Certainly it is the "best" for us now, and it is not only legitimate but laudable for us to foster a spirit of preferential love. I think it was St. Francis de Sales who said: "For us there is no congregation more worthy of love and more desirable than ours, since our Lord has willed that it should be our country and our bark of salvation." To foster this special love of one's own institute is not narrow-mindedness. A young man may have the most profound respect for other women yet very reasonably look upon his own mother as the best in the world. So, too, religious may have great esteem for the members, the customs, and the work of other institutes, yet they prefer and treasure their own above all the others.

The well-ordered love of one's institute will not, however, blind us to its deficiencies or prevent us from trying by legitimate methods to improve its customs. No institute is so perfect as to exclude the need of occasional changes, especially in non-essentials. It is not true loyalty, but sheer obstinacy, that urges us to hold fast to old things just because they are old, or resists any reasonable modification in the habit or any change of customs. Even the general laws of the Church are not so perfect as to exclude change.

Family loyalty will not blind us to the defects of our brethren, but it will certainly prevent us from criticizing either our brethren or our institute to outsiders. These things are family secrets; outsiders have no right to know them. I am referring here to criticism of one's superiors or fellow-religious before the boys or girls in school, before the nurses in training, before the parish priest, or before the men and women in the parish, for example. To reveal to such persons the real faults of the community is detraction, and to misrepresent the community is calumny. Besides, the harm done by such gossip easily assumes serious proportions.

In censuring disloyal speech, I am not thinking of revelations made to canonical visitors or of the unburdening of one's conscience in confession. The canonical visitor is deputed by the Church to ask questions, and in his exercise of this function he is not to be considered an "outsider." The confessor is bound by the most absolute of secrets; and the community is sufficiently protected against harm even when the religious, in explaining his faults or trials, must incidentally refer to the misconduct of others.

Further Practical Suggestions

I have tried to keep my explanation of the constituents of religious family life from being too theoretical, and I hope I have succeeded to some extent. I should like now to increase the practicality of this chapter by suggesting a few concrete ways of contributing to the family spirit of our institutes and communities.

The purpose of a religious institute is to carry on

the work assigned to it by the Church and thus honor God and further His kingdom in the souls of men. In the ordinary providence of God, the supernatural efficiency of the institute depends on its holiness, and this holiness is not some abstract thing; it is, concretely speaking, the sum total of the holiness of the members. Very truly, therefore, each member can say: "The holier I am, the holier is my institute."

This truth should be a source of great inspiration and encouragement to all who are devoted to their religious family, for in the matter of holiness there is no distinction of grade or work. The general, the provincial, the local superior, the teacher, the nurse, the dean, the housekeeper, the cook, the sick, the retired, the contemplative—all have an equal opportunity of promoting the family cause through an increase of holiness. The saintly cook, therefore, makes a much finer contribution to the most exalted purpose of his institute than does the tepid preacher or the worldly teacher.

Holiness, of course, includes the whole of one's life —prayer, work, suffering, everything—but it refers particularly to the interior life of prayer and penance. In these interior practices every religious has great power to help his institute. For one thing, it is the interior spirit that gives the supreme supernatural value to our own work. Moreover, the interior life of one religious can have a tremendous influence on the apostolic work of the others; and it is well for the contemplatives, for those who do the hidden, humble works, and for those who are ill or retired, to note it.

This last point is of the utmost importance, and I should like to illustrate it by a simple example. A priest seldom goes on a mission, rarely enters the confessional, without the realization that he may have to deal with some souls who are "stubborn" or "weak," souls that desperately need superabundant grace for their conversion and salvation. Some of these people seem to have the kind of devil that our Lord said is driven out only by prayer and fasting, yet they themselves are too weak or too callous to do the required prayer and fasting. If they are to be saved, someone must do it for them—at least enough so that they will finally respond to the grace that enables them to carry on for themselves. The priest, despite the best of intentions, cannot do it all.

On occasions like this, I have always rejoiced in the realization that I have a number of friends who gladly offer some of their prayers and sufferings for my apostolate. Shortly after my ordination, I was privileged to meet a saintly nun, Sister Agnesetta, of the Sisters of Loretto. We became fast friends, and she was a great help to me until the day of her death. As a young sister she had been reduced to the state of a helpless cripple. During her last years she could barely lift her tiny knotted hand to blow a whistle when she needed help. Exteriorly she was so cheerful that a casual visitor would think she enjoyed being bedridden. Yet, interiorly, for upwards of twenty years she felt not only the physical pain of her illness but the much greater crucifixion of frustration, of "being on the shelf." I cannot express how much it meant to me to begin an apostolic work with the knowledge that some of her prayers and sufferings were being offered for me.

I have mentioned Sister Agnesetta by name because she has gone to her reward and cannot be embarrassed by my words. I could mention many more of my own and other institutes if they were not still living. And I imagine that every priest could do the same.

What has all this to do with family spirit? The answer, at least as regards active institutes, seems obvious. In the various active institutes, there are teachers who are trying to win wayward pupils, nurses trying to bring about deathbed conversions, preachers who must stir the hearts of hardened sinners, confessors who must draw penitents away from habits of sin. These and others exercising the apostolate need supernatural help. And what is more natural than that they look for this help from the members of their own institute? I do not mean that our vision should not take in the whole Church, with its entire apostolate; I simply mean that our own institute should normally have the first place in our apostolic intentions.

My remaining suggestions will be very brief. First, there is our work. The work of a religious institute is teamwork; it is not the accomplishment of any individual. Each of us contributes to the cause, and it is only by the complete cooperative effort that the desired result is accomplished. In terms of family spirit, this is another consoling truth. It makes each of us realize that his job is *important*.

Then there is charity. The finest act of charity a

religious can show his brethren is good example. All of us know the force of example. How easy it is, for instance, to keep the rule of silence when everyone else observes it; and how difficult it is when even a few neglect it! And, speaking of example, I must at least mention our dealings with externs. They are prone to judge a whole institute by one member; hence each member has a tremendous responsibility to his religious family when he deals with them. The religious with true devotion to his institute will always try to act in the presence of externs in such a way as to cause them to esteem his community and his institute.

Also, as regards charity, there is the matter of mutual correction. The very fact that we are a family gives each of us an added responsibility for the welfare of the others and, of course, for the reputation of the institute. In a family, when one of the children is making a fool out of himself, the other children tell him or their parents about it; and, observing the sound principles of fraternal correction, we religious have to do the same thing. Sometimes religious note that one of their brethren is on the verge of giving great scandal, yet they say nothing either to the individual or to superiors. This is shirking responsibility, a gross form of family disloyalty.

Poverty offers a fertile field for the family spirit. The religious who fully realizes that community life is a sharing enterprise—that "he lives off the community, and the community lives off him," as the saying goes—will not refuse gifts just because he "would have to turn them in," or spend his time calculating how he might add some gift to his super-fluities without sinning seriously against poverty. How would we live if no one were willing to "turn things in"? And in a natural family, would it not be a strange father or mother or sister or brother who would refuse a generous gift with the words, "Really, I don't need it for myself; all I could do with it is give it to the family"?

Religious with a family spirit do not waste things. They do not leave it to someone else to turn off a radiator when heat isn't needed, to close a window when it is letting in too much cold air or when a storm is brewing and floors or furniture would be ruined. They do not acquire books, clothing, and other things that they do not need. In other words, like the members of any poor family, they economize.

Perhaps I should add, by way of parenthesis, that when I speak of the need of economy, I am thinking mostly in terms of men. I have often wondered how we men could get along on sisters' salaries; how we could crowd our books, wardrobes, and various junk boxes into the cells or (more often) dormitories that make up the living quarters of our convents; or how we should look were our clothes subjected to the frequent mendings that give sisters' habits such a long life on this earth.

In my religious life I have heard much about obedience, but after the first few years I seldom heard anything new. A few years ago, however, I did hear a retreat master say something new. At any rate, it was new to me. He said, "The obedient man is the *available* man." This brief statement expresses in a practical, concrete way the whole secret of religious obedience. Our strength lies in the fact that a superior can dispose of us according to the common need; that he can command us, or ask us, or merely suggest to us, and he always finds us ready. We don't shirk a job; we don't dodge responsibility. Few things can be harder for a superior than to have to approach a subject when he knows his request will be greeted by either a growl or an alibi; and I imagine that few things are sweeter for the superior than the realization that his community is composed of *available* subjects, religious who graciously accept any assignment at any time.

One concluding remark. To foster our humility we are often told that if we were gone our place would soon be filled and the community would not even miss us. Perhaps that aspect of our life is sometimes overdone. Perhaps it is good for us to think occasionally of how important we are, of how much we, as individuals, mean to the community. The thought can be very inspiring. I trust that some of the suggestions made here will help to provide this inspiration.

chapter 3

The Particular Friendship

THE novice closed the book, leaned back in his chair, and looked thoughtfully at the ceiling. He had been reading about the friendship of two saints. It was a warm and intimate friendship, yet spiritual writers would surely call it commendable and sanctifying. On the other hand, only a few days before, he had heard a talk on "the particular friendship," and this was definitely branded as reprehensible for religious and an obstacle to their sanctification. What is the difference, he mused, between these two types of friendship? Why is one good, the other bad, for religious? How can one enjoy the benefits of the first while guarding against the evils of the second?

That novice might be any novice. In fact, the puzzled reader of the account of friendship between the saints might well be a religious professed for many years. Experienced spiritual directors say that the question of friendship is a problem for many, if not most, religious. These directors think that the solution to the problem lies in a proper understanding of the particular friendship, and they are of the opinion that an informative psychological discussion of this topic would be helpful to religious. The following notes represent an attempt to treat, or at least to outline, the main points involved in understanding the particular friendship and in avoiding such a friendship or breaking it if one has already been formed.

I. MEANING OF A PARTICULAR FRIENDSHIP

A particular friendship, as the expression is used here, is *an exclusive companionship between two persons which is based on emotional fascination.* In explaining this definition, it may be well first to limit ourselves to some concrete situation: for instance, to a particular friendship between two religious of the same community; or, even more concretely, to such a friendship between two novices. Later, the remarks can easily be applied to other situations.

The definition I have given is a technical one. It is so worded as to exclude certain companionships that are sometimes rather inaccurately styled particular friendships. The clique, for example, is an exclusive companionship; it is limited to a few and excludes others. And because it is exclusive it is harmful to common life. But it is not a particular friendship in the strict sense of the expression because it is not limited to two persons.

Even exclusive companionships between two persons are not necessarily particular friendships in the technical sense. For instance, one pair of novices may

1 The material given here on the particular friendship is largely an adaptation for religious of the general treatment of the sex instinct given in *Modern Youth and Chastity* (St. Louis: Queen's Work, 1943).

be drawn together simply because each dislikes a crowd. Another pair may associate merely because of some mutual hobby—a liking for birds, for flowers, for some game or work. And still another pair may unite for the sole reason that misery loves company; each is, as the saying goes, "agin the government," and their companionship furnishes an outlet for this contrariness. In companionships like these there seems to be no strong emotional binding force; the exclusiveness appears to be the result of purely external circumstances. Of course, associations such as these can easily lead to emotional attachment; but, unless they do so, they are not to be considered particular friendships in the sense in which we are now using the expression.

In the real particular friendship the precise reason for the exclusiveness of the companionship is emotional fascination. The parties conduct themselves much in the manner of young lovers. The whole process of the formation and growth of the friendship follows a rather definite psychological pattern. Religious should be acquainted with the psychology underlying this companionship so that they may protect themselves against tendencies that might otherwise prove very harmful to them.

The Adolescent

It will help towards a better understanding of the particular friendship if we now leave our novitiate setting for a time and take a brief glance at the emotional life of the growing boy. (I choose the boy merely to be more definite. Everything that I say here applies, with the necessary changes of gender, to the growing girl.)

In the years just preceding adolescence the normal boy has very likely limited his close friendships to other boys and has had as little as possible to do with girls. Girls had no attraction for him, except perhaps to arouse his curiosity. But as the weight of adolescence settles upon him, things change. He finds girls mysteriously charming, very attractive; he wants to please them, and he seeks to be a hero in their eyes. Perhaps, even in the very early years of adolescence, he experiences what is popularly called "puppy love"; he may, in fact, have this romantic experience rather frequently. Usually, though not always, these youthful romances are of short duration. There may be great emotional exhilaration for a time; but it is easily exploded, like a child's balloon, and normally has no severe lasting effects.

But as the boy moves on into the upper years of adolescence, it is quite normal for him to center his attraction on one girl; and this experience, though it follows the same pattern as the earlier cases of "puppy love," is more profound. It is this more matured experience that I want to analyze here—to observe its usual manifestations, its origin, and its purpose.

If you were to ask a young man how he happened to fall in love with a certain girl, he might be unable to tell you. And if he could tell you what had suddenly caught his attention and captured his heart, he might answer: "The color of her eyes, the wave of her hair, the way she danced, the special musical quality of her voice"—all apparently trivial things.

[58]

Or perhaps it was an expression of sympathy, a word spoken in his defense, an impression of great virtue—things of greater significance. It is difficult to analyze this first step of falling in love; it is to a great extent mysterious. But the reaction to that first stimulus is not so mysterious. The boy's heart is captured—riveted, as it were, on that one girl. The thought of her tends to absorb his mind; spontaneously he desires to share with her his thoughts, his wishes, his dreams, even his prayers. She has become the center of his emotional life to the exclusion of other girls, and he wants a similar place in her affections. Hence he burns with jealousy if another boy enters into the picture.

Of course, the boy who falls in love still retains his affection for his parents, for his brothers and sisters, and for his boy friends. He may still have a friendly liking for many other girls. But over all these affections—dominating them, as it were—is this one distinctive attraction. If the girl he loves is absent, he suffers torture and feels dissatisfied; he finds it hard to study, to do his work, even to be pleasant to others. He seeks some satisfaction in the possession of little souvenirs, is inclined to telephone, to write frequent and effusive letters, and so forth. When with his beloved, he is overjoyed. He wants to express his affection in sweet words, in kissing and caressing. Incidentally, here lies the great danger to chastity in even the purest courtship. It may be that these manifestations of affection are joined with the deepest reverence; yet they tend to heighten emotion, and thus to increase in frequency, ardor, and physical intimacy.

It is easily seen that if the girl reciprocates the boy's affection, the natural result of the mutual exclusiveness and intensity of their companionship is a complete assimilation of interests. They tend to have the same likes and dislikes. They want to share everything—from the prosaic act of munching the same sandwich to the exchange of the most delicate secrets. In a word, their affection *locks* their hearts together; each is convinced that this state of affairs will last forever, and each craves a complete oneness with the other. They want to blend and share their entire lives.

The experience of falling in love is not something occasional or extraordinary. It has been happening throughout the world since time was young; it is happening now; and it will go on happening, so it seems, till the end of time. Because it is so common, and because it follows such a definite pattern, it seems logical to conclude that the tendency to fall in love is instinctive. I do not mean that everyone has the experience; many factors can intervene to block off the actual experience. But I do mean that, speaking generally, we all have this tendency, an instinctive tendency; and if that is true, it must come from God, and He must have a reason for giving it.

As a matter of fact, it is not difficult to find a very good reason why God should have placed this tendency in human nature. God's plan for the family contains the explanation. In the divine plan for human beings, children are brought into the world as very helpless little things. They develop slowly; they need the care of father and mother for a long time.

God evidently wants the father and mother to live together in the closest intimacy all the days of their lives. This long-continued life together involves many burdens and grave responsibilities towards each other and towards the children. If this kind of life did not have its attractive features as well as its burdens and responsibilities, only the heroes would have the courage to embrace it.

As we know, God does not lay burdens and responsibilities on human nature without also providing compensations. He creates every human being a potential parent, and He also gives each certain capacities and instinctive tendencies that make married life and parenthood not only bearable but attractive. One of these instinctive tendencies is the inclination to an exclusive, tender companionship. This serves as a powerful inducement to marriage; and, after marriage, if this mutual tender love is fostered, it not only provides for the care of the children but also lightens the burdens of the parents and protects them, at least to some extent, from dangers that might come from outside the family circle.

Application to Novices

The foregoing analysis of falling in love suffices for our present purpose. We have answered the questions that seemed fundamental. It is time now to return to our novitiate setting and to apply the conclusions of our psychological analysis to the case of a particular friendship among novices.

The application, it seems to me, should be fairly obvious. A young man enters the novitiate at just

[61]

about the time when this tendency towards exclusive emotional companionship is most likely to manifest itself. That it should manifest itself is perfectly natural. On the other hand, the atmosphere of the novitiate is not perfectly natural: the novice's companionship is limited to members of his own sex. But this fact is not in itself enough to suppress the instinctive yearning for exclusive companionship. Strong appetites have a way of asserting themselves; and, if they cannot find their normal object, they look for a substitute. The novice's tendency to form a particular friendship seems to be an unconscious seeking for such a substitute. That is why the particular friendship exhibits, as was remarked previously, many of the signs of a love affair: exclusiveness, absorbing thoughts, secret meetings, and sentimental demonstrations of affection.

Harmful Effects

From what has been said, it is easily seen how fostering a particular friendship has disastrous effects on the religious life. Its *exclusiveness* renders well-nigh impossible the practice of that universal and impartial charity which is so important for harmony within a religious family and for carrying on apostolic works. The *absorption of mind* on the love-object not only interferes with study and work, but most of all it prevents the union with God that the life of prayer and other spiritual exercises ought to develop.

The third source of danger is the *yearning to manifest one's affection by embraces*. If these cravings are

[62]

satisfied, a great protective barrier to chastity is broken down, and serious sins can result. Moreover, once this barrier is broken by familiarities, it is rebuilt only with great difficulty. I might mention here that this danger is probably greater in a friendship between two women than in a similar friendship between men. Men are protected to some extent by the consciousness that kissing and embracing are not customary among the members of their sex, whereas among women it is more natural to express even ordinary affection in such ways.

Embracing, of course, is not the only source of danger to chastity. Other little familiarities can also break down reserve and open the way to temptation. And even when external modesty is preserved, the emotional friendship can be a source of great disturbance to the imagination. Daydreams will not always remain on the spiritual plane.

Not Limited to Novices

Although the particular friendship, in the full sense in which we have described it, is hardly of frequent occurrence among religious, the tendency to form this association is certainly common enough to warrant a thorough discussion of the subject. And this tendency is not limited to novices. In fact, the possible combinations in which the particular friendship might appear are quite varied. For instance, two religious of about the same age, both of whom have been professed for several years, might form such an attachment while teaching or carrying on some other apostolic work. The dangers in this case are generally much more grave than they would be in the noviti- ate because of the greater opportunity of indulging the affection.

Then there is the possibility of a particular friend- ship between a young religious (perhaps a novice or a recently professed religious) and an older one. It is difficult to overestimate the possible harmful effects of this relationship, especially for the young reli- gious. Indeed, a very promising vocation can be lost in this way. The young religious is unwarily drawn into the affair, loses interest in spiritual exercises, suffers perhaps many grievous temptations against chastity, and at last, with former high ideals of reli- gious perfection completely shattered, returns to the world. An older religious who would take the initia- tive in a companionship of this kind, or willingly en- courage it, would be running a risk of giving grave scandal. Fortunately ignorance excuses from guilt; but such ignorance should not be perpetually fostered.

Again, the particular friendship is not limited to the religious family. An extern may be one of the parties. It is not entirely uncommon for a pupil to develop what is sometimes referred to as a "crush" on the teacher. If the teacher also loses emotional control, there results the particular friendship of the teacher-pupil variety. This topic is usually treated rather thoroughly by the psychologists of adolescence. Many adolescents develop these "crushes" on their elders. These young people, we must remember, are still in the transitional period; their emotional life is just developing and it will go on developing if nothing happens to fix it at a childish level. Thus, one of the great evils of the teacher-pupil particular friendship is the retardation of emotional development in the pupil.

This is a difficult situation to handle, as anyone will admit. In some instances it may require a sort of self-crucifixion for the teacher because the teacher may be very fond of the child and may have a deep yearning for the child's affection. But if this yearning is satisfied by reciprocating the pupil's attentions (and much more so by taking the initiative in seeking attentions), a very harmful situation arises. The pupil's own emotional growth is stunted, as we mentioned above; and scandal is given to others because of the partiality which is usually shown and because of the out-and-out childishness that a teacher sometimes manifests in such circumstances. Youth has a right to expect better emotional control of us.

Yet, even if the teacher's own emotions are perfectly under control, the handling of the adolescent "crush" is a delicate matter. As it is unfair to the pupil for the teacher to initiate these emotional attachments or to respond emotionally to them, so it seems equally damaging to deal harshly with such a pupil. The teacher has to be both objective and kind. Luella Cole, in her books *Psychology of Adolescence* [2] and *The Background for College Teaching*,[3] suggests three principles for the teacher to follow on these occasions. The first principle is one we have already indicated: namely, the teacher should never show emotional interest in the pupil. The second principle

2 New York: Farrar & Rinehart, 1942; pp. 147-149.
3 New York: Farrar & Rinehart, 1940; pp. 164-165.

[65]

is to avoid being alone with the student, especially behind closed doors, because it is then that the emotions are most likely to run riot. The third principle is to provide the devoted student (whether boy or girl) with plenty of work. The author suggests such physical activities as cleaning erasers and washing blackboards, and, with special reference to the college student, some mental occupation such as special work in the library. It is her opinion that several weeks of these physical or mental tasks will be sufficient to cool the ardor of the student. Her suggestions seem very helpful. The one precaution that might be added here is that in assigning work the teacher should guard against giving the appearance of favoritism.

Perhaps what I have written about the teacher-pupil attachment was a digression; yet I believe it is not wholly without pertinence. Moreover, the remarks made with reference to this relationship are also applicable to other situations in which religious deal with youth. Similar attachments can be formed; similar dangers are present; and similar precautions and treatment are necessary.

We can conclude the enumeration of the various situations that may occasion a particular friendship by referring briefly to the most obvious, though fortunately not the most common, case—namely, the possibility of falling in love with a person of the opposite sex. In their early years of training, religious are usually protected from this danger, at least to a great extent, by the fact that they do not associate much with externs. And even in later years, when they are engaged in works of the apostolate, they are somewhat protected by the ordinary regimentation and supervision of their lives. They would be safeguarded still more if the provisions for cloister, companions, and external reserve were always rigorously observed. But nothing save a special grace of God can protect them to the point of utter immunity. As human beings they are always susceptible to such attachments.

A very realistic professor of pastoral theology used to tell his seminarians: "In your priestly lives you will often have to deal with women. In some cases you will necessarily be alone with them. If, on one of these occasions, a woman should burst into tears, do not yield to the impulse to dry them for her." This is a rather concrete way of saying that one must not let sympathy interfere with judgment. Even spiritual ministries and apostolic works can be very dangerous, especially when sympathy plays on the heartstrings. A prudent reserve is always called for if one wants to keep his heart where he placed it at the time of his consecration to God—in the Heart of Christ.

Ordinary Friendship

After hearing a discourse on the particular friendship, a young religious is apt to be confused. "What does it all mean? Am I supposed to have no intimate friends? Must I keep my heart in solitary confinement?"

The answer to such questions, whether spoken or unspoken, should be very straightforward. True friendship is one of the great blessings of life, and it belongs to religious just as much as to others.

Father Tanquerey, after treating of the benefits of true friendship, writes the following pertinent paragraph:

The question has been asked whether or not such friendships should be encouraged in *communities*. It may be feared that they will be detrimental to the affection which should unite all the members and that they will be the cause of jealousies. Assuredly, care must be taken that such friendships do not interfere with the charity due to all, that they be supernatural and be kept within the limits set by Superiors. With these provisions, friendship retains in communities all the advantages described above, since religious as well as others need the counsel, comfort and protection that a friend alone can give. However, in communities more than elsewhere, all that savors of false friendship must be avoided with jealous care.[4]

Certainly the lives of religious who became canonized saints furnish ample proof that genuine friendship is not at variance with the ideals of the religious life. These saints had intimate friends within their communities and outside their communities, friends among those of their own sex and friends of the opposite sex. Moreover, the mere reading of some of their letters indicates that their friendships were warm and affectionate. And we need not confine ourselves to the lives of canonized saints, as if true friendship were a prerogative of heroic sanctity. Very likely most religious who are now in the declining years of life could tell us that the friendships they have

4 *The Spiritual Life* (Tournai: Desclée, 2nd ed., 1930), n. 599.

formed have been a source of great joy in their lives and of much help in the service of God.

The essential difference apparently lies in quality: one kind of friendship is good for religious, another kind is harmful. With regard to human companionship, there is one sense in which religious must go to God alone; another sense in which companionship, intimate companionship, is not only permissible, but helpful.

How to Distinguish

"But," the young religious will ask, "how can one judge whether a friendship is just ordinary friendship or a particular friendship?" The simplest way of making this distinction is to examine a companionship to see if it manifests the specific signs of the particular friendship.

One specific characteristic of the particular friendship is its *exclusiveness*. Ordinary friendship is not exclusive. Because of circumstances or because of his own temperament, a religious may possibly have only one good friend, but this is not of the nature of ordinary friendship. One person can have many good friends.

The exclusive tendency of the particular friendship easily breeds *jealousy*. The fact that one's friend has other friends is resented. Ordinary friendship does not have this effect; it allows freedom not only for oneself but for one's friend in the choice of other friends.

The particular friendship is marked by internal

[69]

absorption of mind on the friend. The thoughts and affections are, as it were, bound to one person: internal freedom to pray, to study, to work, to be with other companions, to brook separation, is hampered. Ordinary friendship, on the other hand, does not greatly interfere with this freedom. I say "not greatly" because it seems to me that one cannot, without qualification, apply to ordinary friendship the dictum "Out of sight, out of mind." Even the truest and most spiritual of friendships is not as cold as that. Perhaps it would be more accurate to say that in the particular friendship internal adjustment to separation is extraordinarily difficult, whereas in the case of the simple friendship it is comparatively easy.

Finally, the tendency to *manifest affection* by soft words and embraces arises spontaneously when a particular friendship is fostered. This is not a distinctive characteristic of ordinary friendship. It is true, of course, that some people are much more externally affectionate than others; true also that a certain amount of external demonstration is more natural with women than with men. Nevertheless, these things are not characteristic marks of the simple friendship; an unusual tendency to such manifestations is a sign that something other than ordinary friendship is involved.

To sum the matter up negatively: ordinary friendship does not interfere with the common life, with impartial charity, with prayer, with the performance of one's duty, with the prudent reserve that must characterize the bearing of religious. Again, briefly, but still negatively: any friendship which does not interfere with the attainment of religious ideals is a sound friendship. Finally, to put it positively: any friendship which helps one to lead a good religious life is not only safe and permissible, but actually a gift of God.

About Inversion

Some readers may have wondered why my explanation of the particular friendship among religious did not mention sexual inversion as a possible cause. I omitted this because I think most of the cases can be reasonably explained without reference to the abnormal. However, I admit that occasionally the attraction of one religious to another may be a manifestation of an inverted sexual instinct; hence, a few words on this subject seem called for.[5]

The normal object of the sexual instinct is the opposite sex, as I have already explained. However, there are some people who are not normal: they are attracted, not to the opposite sex, but to their own. Such people are said to be sexually inverted, or homosexual. The latter word, by the way, is a perfectly innocent scientific term that has become opprobrious because of its frequent application to persons who are morally degenerate. The reading of popular journals might easily lead one to think that homosexuals are always involved in sins against chastity. This is not true. Some inverts are people of very noble character who practice heroic virtue while leading a life that is generally very lonely. The mere fact that one

[5] A wholesome and practical book on this subject is *The Invert*, by Anomaly (London: Bailliere, Tindall & Cox, 1948).

is sexually attracted—whether psychologically, physically, or both—to a person of one's own sex is no necessary sign of homosexuality. But if this attraction is experienced regularly even in situations in which one associates with members of the opposite sex, and if, in these same situations, there is no attraction to the oposite sex—this is usually a sign of an inverted instinct. In other words, homosexuality implies: (a) sexual attraction to one's own sex, (b) no such attraction to the opposite sex, and (c) this in circumstances in which there is association with members of both sexes.

It is not for me to go into the various theories about homosexuality. It suffices to say in general that, according to the best scholars, the reason for the inversion may be innate (e.g., in the endocrine glands), or it may be in one's development (e.g., some external circumstance that retarded the normal progression of the sexual instinct), or it may be a combination of these things. Whatever be the explanation, it is safe to say that, while the condition exists, it is not wise to marry and it would seldom be wise to enter religion. Consequently, if a vocational counselor knew that a candidate for the religious life was homosexual, he would almost always advise him to give up the idea of becoming a religious; and if a director found that the reason for a particular friendship in religion, or for a persistently strong inclination to such a friendship, was an inverted instinct, he would often advise the person to leave religion. But, as I said, I think that the more usual explanation of the particular friendship among religious lies rather in

[72]

the fact that the persons are basically normal but there is no association with the other sex. That is what I have stressed, and what I shall now say about the remedies supposes this to be the case.

II. REMEDIES FOR THE PARTICULAR FRIENDSHIP

In a general way, the problem of restraining any unwholesome emotional reaction involves some or all of the following factors. One should not dodge his problem, but should face it squarely. One must realize that, at least for him, the expression of this emotion is really undesirable—a genuine evil, or at least a hindrance to a great good. In controlling the emotion, one should avoid everything that stimulates it, insofar as this is reasonably possible; and, if the stimuli themselves are unavoidable, the impulses to foster the emotion should then be restrained. It is particularly advisable that this avoidance of stimuli and restraining of impulses should be accomplished calmly, without fear and worry. And, whenever possible, some positive, wholesome substitute for the undesirable emotion should be cultivated.

These general suggestions should be kept in mind in solving any problem. In applying them to the question of the particular friendship, it is necessary to visualize two distinct cases and to treat these cases separately. The first case concerns a person who has not yet formed a particular friendship but who feels a strong tendency towards doing so. In the religious life this would be the more common, and the less difficult, problem. The second case concerns one who has already formed a particular friendship. Because of the great difficulties presented by this latter case, we shall consider it first. For the safe of clarity, our remarks will be grouped round these keywords: *conviction, confidence, general self-discipline, physical separation, mental separation,* and *other interests.*

Breaking a Friendship

By *conviction* I mean realization of values—sincere, deep motivation. No one will attempt to restrain a strong and pleasant affection unless he really sees that it is undesirable and unless he really wants to restrain it. An unconvinced and halfhearted man will do nothing that calls for effort and sacrifice. Moreover, when there is question of a personal emotional problem, *mere* argument is generally useless. I have previously outlined many harmful, even disastrous, effects of the particular friendship. It hurts prayer, interferes with work, is a nuisance to social life within a community, leads to a loss of ideals, presents a source of danger to chastity, and may even culminate in a loss of vocation. In fine, at its best, it blocks off true progress in the love of God; at its worst, it can lead to hell.

These various effects of the particular friendship are well-known to everyone who has had to deal with such cases. Nevertheless, the religious who is involved in a particular friendship is apt to hear or read a recital of these evils without being much affected. He is in the same mental state as the Catholic who knows his faith perfectly yet, blinded by love, runs off with a divorced person. Such people will not be convinced, in the real sense of the word, without humble, prolonged prayer. They have to see, even to *feel,* with the aid of what I might call the warming grace of God, that these arguments apply to them. They have to fight love with love. The love involved in their human attachment conflicts with the love they owe to our Lord. Compromise in this matter is an impossibility; they cannot have both loves.

Real conviction, therefore, results in a desire to break a particular friendship. But desire in itself is not enough. One must also have *confidence* that this can be done. No one will attempt to do what he really judges to be impossible; and, when the emotions have been captivated, one naturally and quite spontaneously feels helpless to adjust them.

One way of counteracting this feeling of helplessness is the practice of the too-much-neglected virtue of hope. We have our Lord's solemn promise that He will give us the graces necessary for doing His will; and we have the examples of the saints and of everyday experience to prove that those who stretch out their hands to Him and cooperate with His grace can do almost incredibly heroic things. It is hardly necessary to dwell here on the examples of great conversions among the saints, but it may be helpful to insist on the fact that daily experience proves that those who sincerely want to control even the strongest emotions can do so. Religious themselves, as guides of young people, frequently have to urge them to break off some unsuitable courtship. Many lose heart and do not follow the advice, but many others do follow it and succeed. What they can do, religious can surely do, especially since religious have such easy access to supernatural helps.

The third key word is *general self-discipline*. The organization called Alcoholics Anonymous, which has achieved remarkable results in the rehabilitation of persons addicted to alcoholism, has capitalized on this point—as, indeed, it has capitalized on almost the entire program outlined here. The alcoholic's attention is not wholly concentrated on his one central problem, as if he were a saint except for that; he is directed to make an inventory of all his faults and to begin a *complete* reform by general self-discipline. This is sound psychology and sound asceticism, too; and the religious who faces the problem of breaking a particular friendship would do well to follow it.

To speak concretely, the whole spiritual life must be tuned up: observance of the Rule, application to duty, control of temper, and so on. The *regular* practice of prayer and of small mortifications is especially important. An integrated program like this has the natural advantage of giving general control over feelings and impulses, and the supernatural advantage of winning the special grace necessary for victory in the central problem—namely, the breaking of the friendship.

The first direct attack on the friendship itself is the blocking off of all unnecessary stimuli to the emotion. Evidently this includes some degree of *physical separation*. At the very minimum, private meetings must cease; and really severe cases can hardly be cured without complete physical separation, which implies a change of residence for one of

[76]

the parties.[6] Obviously, a change of residence cannot be effected without the cooperation of the superior; and, when a subject frankly approaches a superior on a matter of this kind, the superior should be sympathetic and as helpful as circumstances permit. Harshness with a subject who has spontaneously asked for help is certainly inexcusable. Sometimes, of course, a change of residence is impossible, at least temporarily; and sometimes it is not necessary because the friendship is not far enough advanced to call for such a drastic measure.

Physical separation alone will not accomplish the desired result: there must also be *mental separation*. There should be no letter writing; and little souvenirs such as pictures, notes, and old leters, should be destroyed. Then, with these external reminders out of the way, the next step is to purify the imagination of its tendency to dwell fondly on "the good old times." This involves the same problem that is encountered in any attempt to rid the mind of persistent undesirable thoughts.

The preceding steps are largely negative; they are designed to empty the mind and the heart of the troublesome attachment. But one cannot preserve a

6 When I say that severe cases may call for a change of residence I do not wish to imply that an even greater change might not occasionally be required. Cases may occur in which one or both parties manifest either an excessive and very dangerous lack of emotional control or even an abnormally directed instinct. In such instances the good of the individual and especially the common good may call for a change, not merely of residence, but of vocation. In the text I am supposing the existence of a genuine vocation and am simply giving the remedies for a temporary emotional difficulty.

[77]

vacuum of soul. One must love something and be interested in something. Hence, the final step is the cultivation of *other interests*. At first this is very difficult, for loneliness, moodiness, and a distaste for other persons and things are the natural reactions to an effort to break a particular friendship. One must not, however, succumb to such unwholesome reactions. This is not the time to indulge a martyr complex by volunteering for the foreign missions; rather, it is the time to learn to appreciate the interesting things, the enjoyable companionships, and the profitable labors that are right at hand. Wholesome friendships and a more intensified love of God, manifested by a willingness to work and to take part in common recreations and entertainments—things like these will dispel the gloom and readjust the violently shaken emotions.

Such in general is the program for breaking a particular friendship. The second case to be considered concerns the person who has not formed such a friendship but who feels strongly attracted towards doing so.

Restraining an Attraction

Perhaps the most fundamental rule to be observed by a religious when he first feels a strong exclusive attraction towards another is this: *Do not be surprised*. In this connection, I might mention the very effective technique followed by a certain wise spiritual director in quieting young religious who were unnecessarily worried over the fact that they experienced temptations against chastity. He would begin by asking his worried consultant:

"On a fast day, don't you ever feel hungry at about ten or eleven o'clock in the morning?"

"Why, of course," would be the inevitable answer.

"And do you get surprised or worried?"

"Of course not," the equally inevitable answer.

"Then, why should you be surprised at these temptations? You are denying a very strong appetite. These strong urges that you feel are merely signs of its hunger."

This same reasoning may be applied to the longing for intimate, exclusive companionship. God gave everyone this yearning. The religious has renounced its fulfillment in favor of a greater good; yet, in renouncing the right to satisfy the yearning, the religious has not destroyed the yearning itself, and he should not be surprised if it makes itself felt at times in regard to some person either of his own or of the opposite sex.

The first rule, therefore, is to keep calm and to remember, "I'm fasting." Then, very quietly but firmly, one should see that he does not foster the exclusive attraction in any way: by needless thinking of the other person, private meetings, or special signs of affection. Let him be faithful to the common life, to the practice of universal charity, to his work, and to his prayer. As his mind tends to be absorbed with thoughts of the one person, let him quietly try to replace these by other thoughts.

It is highly desirable that a religious who is undergoing this trial should be perfectly frank with his spiritual director or with his superior, or with both. The young religious is liable to fear this: he is prone to think that he may be considered singular. Such fears are vain. If he is singular, then to be human is singular. It is very helpful, if not absolutely necessary, to be able to unburden one's soul in these human difficulties; for even if the spiritual director or the superior can do little more than listen sympathetically, the soul is cheered and encouraged.

Occasionally a religious who does not wish to talk over his difficulty with the superior or the spiritual director feels a strong impulse to talk it over with the person towards whom he is attracted. This impulse is to be suspected; it is very likely just a subtle manifestation of the very tendency that is worrying him. It is a type of self-manifestation that can do no good, but much harm; at the very least it is likely to lead to distressing embarrassment.

It sometimes happens that in a friendship that is otherwise very wholesome and beneficial one party begins to experience the tendencies characteristic of the particular friendship. What is to be done in a case like this? A very brief answer to this question might be, "Don't be surprised or worried, but do be careful." It is certainly not necessary to break the friendship immediately; but on the other hand it is necessary to take precautions. In the words of Father Tanquerey: "One must first of all forego what would foster sentiment, like frequent and affectionate conversations, familiarity, etc. From time to time one must deny oneself meetings otherwise in order, and be willing to shorten conversations that cease to be useful. In this way one gains control of sentiment and wards off danger." [7]

Conclusion

It is hardly necessary to mention, by way of conclusion, that extremist attitudes are to be avoided. One should not make too little of the particular friendship, for it does present a real danger, and few religious, if any, can safely consider themselves immune from it in all its forms. It is true that advancing age does diminish liability, yet who can set the definite age at which falling in love ceases to be a possibility?

On the other hand, the problem should not be exaggerated. It is unwise to raise the cry "particular friendship!" merely because two people have been rather frequently seen together. It is also unwise to look upon this as the *only type* of harmful companionship; for there are many other damaging associations, in which little or no sentiment is involved. Finally, it is not wise to guide oneself according to a policy of undue fear and to shun all friendship in order to avoid a particular friendship. In companionships, as in other matters, virtue follows the middle course. And the plan for the middle course seems to be this: avoid unwholesome friendships entirely, and purify wholesome friendships of unwholesome tendencies.

[7] *Op. cit.*, n. 606.

PART II

Fraternal Charity

It is hardly an exaggeration to say that the most important aspect of community life is fraternal charity. Religious communities in which the spirit of fraternal charity is lively usually attract many candidates and have a thriving interior life and a fruitful apostolate.

Discussion of fraternal charity may be predominantly negative or positive. Negative discussions stress the faults against charity; positive discussions emphasize the practice of the virtue. And, as regards the practice of the virtue, one may consider the duties or the ideals. Since the religious life is a quest for perfection, its aim is certainly more than the mere fulfillment of duty; it specializes—if I may use the word—in going beyond the call of duty. And certainly, in the matter of fraternal charity, which our Lord Himself has made the special mark of His followers, the aim of the religious life and of each individual religious ought to be very high. Nevertheless, the first step in the attainment of any ideal is the fulfillment of duty; it is vain to speak of acting beyond the call of duty when duty itself is neglected.

These two chapters on fraternal charity are mainly concerned with duties. Years of experience have convinced me that a clear knowledge of these duties is essential to the proper practice of fraternal charity in religion. In the first place, this knowledge makes for great peace of mind by enabling one to distinguish between what is sinful and what is not. And secondly, as I have indicated in the chapters themselves, this knowledge also shows that the ultimate solution to some of the very acute problems of community life cannot be found on the plane of mere duty; it is found only on the higher plane of perfectly Christ-like living.

chapter 4

The Duty of Loving the Neighbor, Especially Enemies

In explaining the general precept of fraternal charity, theologians usually call attention to the fact that this duty includes all neighbors, even enemies; nevertheless, because our Lord Himself saw fit to voice a special precept regarding the love of enemies and because this duty has special difficulties, the manuals of moral theology usually include an explicit treatment of the duty of loving enemies. These treatises contain much that is practical not only for the ordinary Catholic but also for religious. The purpose of the present notes is to outline the commonly accepted teaching on the duty of loving one's neighbor, particularly one's enemies, and to comment more in detail on points that seem to be of especially practical value to religious.

I. THE GENERAL PRECEPT OF CHARITY

There are many specific duties of fraternal charity: for example, almsgiving, fraternal correction, the avoidance of scandal and of cooperation in another's sin, and the love of enemies. But all these duties are derived from the general precept of fraternal charity, which may be briefly stated as follows: *By divine precept, we must love all our neighbors with the love of charity; and this duty extends to thoughts, words, and deeds.* A brief explanation of this general law may contain a number of helpful points and will clear the ground for a more detailed consideration of the command to love one's enemies.

Charity

Charity is a special kind of love, a supernatural love which is directed primarily to God. By charity we love God for *Himself* because, as we know Him through faith, He is infinitely worthy of love. Genuine charity towards the neighbor is also a love for God because the neighbor, as known through faith, shares in distinctively divine perfections—for example, the divine life of grace and the divine destiny of seeing God face to face.

It is important to note that fraternal charity takes its motive from faith; it sees the neighbor through the eyes of faith. Through faith we know that the neighbor participates, or is called to participate, in the divine life of grace, that he is destined for the beatific vision, that Christ has identified Himself with the neighbor, that the exemplar of true fraternal charity is Christ Himself, that Christ has told us to love our neighbor as He has loved us, and that we are all united through Christ in God. Because of the supernatural bond by which God unites men to

Himself, we love one another with the same kind of love with which we love God—theological charity. Fraternal charity, therefore, is immeasurably superior to all merely natural love, even the noblest. This does not mean, of course, that there is any conflict between natural love and charity. A man's good qualities can be recognized by reason, and he can be reasonably and nobly loved for these. Such reasonable love, furthermore, can easily be supernaturalized and absorbed, so to speak, in the greater love of charity when we see the neighbor's lovable qualities as reflections of the divine goodness.

Who Is My Neighbor?

In answering the lawyer's question with the parable of the Good Samaritan, our Lord did not wish to say that the priest and the levite who scorned the afflicted man were not really his neighbors; rather, He wished to bring out graphically the fact that the only one who really acted like a neighbor was the foreigner, the Samaritan, who bound up his wounds and supplied his needs. Christian tradition, which is the best interpreter of our Lord's words, has always understood the word "neighbor" (in the precept "Love thy neighbor as thyself") to mean all men. In fact, the word includes everyone who has a common destiny with us: men on earth, the souls in purgatory, the blessed in heaven, and (in some sense) even the angels. Among rational and intelligent creatures, only the damned are excluded from the notion of neighbor, because their damnation has forever severed the tie that bound them to us. All others are our neighbors and are objects for our charity. However, the *commandment* is usually understood to refer particularly to men on earth.

Thought, Word, and Deed

The commandment of love includes internal and external acts: thoughts, words, and deeds. And like most commandments it has its negative and its affirmative aspects: that is, it forbids certain things, and it commands certain things. It would be impossible to give here anything approaching a complete enumeration of the duties of charity, because charity is a very general virtue which affects all our attitudes towards and dealings with our neighbor. I can give here only a few general rules which may help individuals in estimating their own duties as regards fraternal charity.

A *negative* rule—that is, a formula expressing what we must not do—is best expressed in terms of the golden rule. Such a formula would run somewhat as follows: Abstain from all deliberate thoughts, words, and actions which you think you would reasonably resent if you were in your neighbor's place. (For a more complete explanation of this rule with regard to speech, see the next chapter.)

On the *affirmative* side, the key word for charity of thought is "well-wishing." Charity is a love of benevolence, that is, of unselfish and disinterested well-wishing; hence, an internal act of fraternal charity is an act of supernatural well-wishing. Such an act can be expressed in many ways: for example, by praying

[88]

for the neighbor's salvation; by rejoicing over his good fortune, especially growth in virtue; by sorrowing over his misfortune, especially sin, and by making internal acts of reparation for the sins of others; by desiring the true happiness of our neighbor; or by being prepared to relieve his needs for the love of God. Even the natural compassion we are apt to feel for those who suffer temporal loss and misfortune and the spontaneous joy we feel over the temporal good fortune of a friend may be implicitly included in and supernaturalized by charity, provided the proper subordination to eternal values is not set aside.

That we are obliged to make such internal acts of charity as I have just enumerated is the unhesitating teaching of Catholic theology. The Church has condemned the opinion that we can fulfill all our duties of charity by merely external acts.

But how often must we make such acts? To that question the best theologian cannot give a definite answer. All that can be said regarding the *obligation* is that such acts must be made *occasionally*. However, though the obligation itself is vague as to frequency, theologians generally agree that it is practically impossible for one who is trying to lead a good Catholic life to fail in this duty. As for what is *advisable,* all theologians would surely agree that frequent acts of fraternal charity should be highly recommended. As a matter of fact, the prayers that are universally recommended for daily recital contain at least two acts of fraternal charity: namely, the act of love and the Our Father.

[89]

Speaking of prayer for the neighbor, the question might be asked: Must we pray for individual neighbors? The general law of charity does not demand this, although certain special relationships such as ties of blood may do so. The general law of charity is fulfilled if we include all our neighbors in our acts of love; or, to put the matter in another way, it suffices if we exclude no one from those acts which, as mentioned above, must be made occasionally. Hence, we may formulate this brief rule for satisfying the general precept to make internal acts of fraternal charity: say the act of love occasionally and mean it, or say the Our Father now and then and exclude no one from its petitions.

What about words and deeds? When are we obliged to manifest our love for our neighbor by speech and action? The key word here is "need"; and a brief rule epitomizing our duties to perform external acts of charity may be stated thus: I am obliged to help my neighbor (corporally or spiritually) when he really needs my help and when I can give the help without a proportionate inconvenience to myself.

It should be noted that this rule expresses only the Christian minimum; namely, the duty, under pain of sin, of performing the works of mercy. The Christian ideal, which was Christ's glory and which has ever been the Church's glory, goes much higher and helps the needy even to the point of utter selflessness and heroism.

As regards the external manifestation of charity, theologians usually lay great stress on the necessity of showing what they call "the common signs of good

will." The explanation of this matter is best reserved for the section of this chapter dealing with the
love of enemies.

The Divine Command

The jottings contained in the previous paragraphs
explain the meaning and the extent of the general
law of fraternal charity. To complete them we might
ask and answer the question: Why must we love one
another? The answer is derived from both reason
and faith.

Reason tells us that, even if God had not raised
man to a supernatural status, we should have some
obligation to love one another. For even in the natural order men would be united by a common nature
and a common destiny; moreover, being social by
nature, they would have to live and work and recreate together. Because of these facts, the natural
law itself, which is perceived by reason, calls for
some love and union, especially for the well-being of
human nature: that is, in order that men may live
together with the degree of harmony which is really
helpful to the attainment of their purpose on earth.

As a matter of fact, we do not live in a purely natural order. Through faith we know that God has given
us a share in His own life (sanctifying grace) and the
destiny of sharing in His own happiness (the beatific
vision). We enjoy an entirely special union with God
in Christ, and the necessary preservative of this union
is charity.

Scriptural texts on fraternal charity can be multi-
plied almost without end. Some of these texts are, it

seems, merely counsels, but many of them evidently state a real precept to love the neighbor. Our Lord referred to fraternal charity as the second great commandment (Matthew 22:39); and St. John said, "This commandment we have from God, that he who loves God must also love his neighbor" (I John 4:21).

As regards external charity in particular, the classic texts are the account of the Last Judgment (see Matthew 25:42), in which our Lord clearly indicates that the attainment of salvation will depend on helping the needy; and the strong words of St. John: "He that hath the substance of this world and shall see his brother in need and shall shut up his bowels from him, how doth the charity of God abide in him?" (I John 3:17-18).

II. THE LOVE OF ENEMIES

That the love of enemies is included in the precept of charity and is in some sense a special sign of the true follower of Christ is indicated by our Lord's words: "But I say to you: love your enemies, do good to them that hate you, and pray for them that persecute and calumniate you; that you may be the children of your Father who is in heaven, who maketh his sun to rise upon the good and the bad, and raineth upon the just and the unjust. For if you love them that love you, what reward shall you have? Do not even the publicans this? And if you salute your brethren only, what do you more? Do not also the heathens this?" (Matthew 5:44-47).

Many other texts of Scripture have a similar meaning. Even the Old Testament has some beautiful passages on the love of enemies and some moving examples of forgiveness. That forgiveness in particular is enjoined on us is apparent from the Our Father and from our Lord's answer to Peter, which He illustrated with the story of the unforgiving servant and concluded with the strong words, "So also shall my heavenly Father do to you [namely, deliver you over to the torturers] if you forgive not everyone his brother from your hearts" (Matthew 18:35).

This divine precept is clearly in accord with man's social nature. We are all prone to offend; and, if it were permissible to nourish hatred and a spirit of revenge and to deny pardon, progressive social peace would be extremely difficult, even impossible. One needs only to glance at history to see the disastrous effects that inevitably flow from hatred and revenge.

General Observations

Who is my enemy? In its primary meaning the term refers to anyone who has offended me, whether by causing me needless sorrow, by insulting me, or by causing me some harm such as a bodily injury, a loss of reputation, or property damage. In a wider sense, my enemy is anyone who dislikes me, or anyone whom I dislike or for whom I feel aversion. The principles of moral theology which will be explained in this section refer mainly to an enemy in the primary sense; but they also apply, and with even greater force, to an enemy in the secondary meaning of the word.

We are not bound to love enemies because they are enemies but *in spite of the fact that* they are enemies.

[93]

In other words, enemies should be loved for the same reason that other neighbors must be loved: namely, because of the common ties, natural and supernatural, that bind us together in God.

Although there is a special precept to love enemies, this does not normally oblige us to show them a special love; the precept simply insists that even enemies may not be excluded from the general duty of charity.

Obviously, the precept of loving one's neighbor does not refer to a *sensible* love. Since this kind of love is not under the free direction of the will, it is not even of obligation with regard to God, parents, or children. The love prescribed is the supernatural love of internal and external benevolence. It is of particular importance to keep this in mind when we are speaking of the love of enemies, because in this matter more than in most others the feelings are apt to cause trouble.

Another observation of practical value: to love one's enemy is not the same as approving of his unlovable qualities. If an enemy sins, we may hate his sin and wish for his correction. If he has repulsive habits, we may, within the scope of well-ordered charity, take means to have him correct those habits.

The precept of loving our enemies imposes upon us the same duties of thought, word, and action that were explained in the notes dealing with the general precept. However, because of the special difficulties involved, moral treatises on the love of enemies usually lay stress on these three specific duties: (a) to put aside hatred and a desire for private and ill-ordered revenge, (b) to show the common signs of good will, (c) and to do what is required to bring about a reconciliation.

Hatred and Revenge

I have read many treatises on hatred; and my candid impression is that the more lengthy they are, the more confusing they become. I will content myself, therefore, with saying that a good practical definition of hatred is: to wish one's neighbor an evil that is not duly subordinated to some good. It is certainly hatred, therefore, to wish an enemy spiritual harm: to wish, for example, that he remain in sin, that he lose his soul, and so forth, for such harm cannot be properly subordinated to any good.

Theoretically, it is not hatred to wish someone a temporal evil for his own good: for example, to wish him sickness or financial misfortune as a means of reforming him. But theologians wisely caution against fostering such thoughts, as they can readily be a form of self-deception when they concern those we dislike.

Revenge is punishment for an offense committed. Ordinarily speaking, revenge belongs to one in authority, and it is wrong for private individuals to take or to plan to take revenge. However, theologians reasonably consider that this rule admits of exception in minor matters: for example, a boy might justly punish another boy for insulting his sister.

Insofar as punishment may be justly inflicted for offenses, it is permissible to wish that such punishment be visited upon an enemy; but dwelling on such thoughts is dangerous, because it can easily develop an unforgiving spirit and even lead to unreasonable desires of punishment.

After suffering an offense, we usually feel "all hot inside," and our imaginations conjure up many evils that we should like to inflict or to have inflicted on our offenders. In themselves, these thoughts are spontaneous and involuntary, and are therefore sinless. They become sins of hatred and revenge only when they are deliberate and when they include the wishing of unjustifiable evil to our enemy. However, protracted brooding over offenses or over the bad qualities of an enemy, even when no actual evil is desired, is a dangerous pastime. At the very least, it disturbs digestion—and, of course, it makes it all the more difficult to fulfill our external duties to our enemies.

The Common Signs of Good Will

A second duty that calls for particular consideration when enemies are concerned is that of showing "the common signs of good will." By these common signs are meant the little courtesies that are ordinarily shown to all men, or at least to all of a certain group. Among these we may mention returning a greeting, answering a question, buying and selling in a public store, replying to letters, tipping one's hat to ladies, showing some sign of respect to superiors, and helping one who is in need.[1] The idea here—which seems so obvious that it is difficult to express in words—is that such courtesies are not normally reserved to

[1] For an application of this material to the important problem of race relations, see Chapter 17.

one's intimate friends but are extended to our neighbors because they are fellow citizens, fellow students, fellow workmen, and the like. In a word, these common signs are different from the kindnesses and attentions that are normally shown only to one's friends —such as inviting them to dinner, having them as guests over the weekend, confiding secrets, carrying on an intimate correspondence, and visiting them when they are ill. These latter are called special signs of good will precisely because they generally indicate some relationship which is especially intimate.

The principle to be kept in mind here is this: we are ordinarily obliged to show the common signs of good will even to our enemies; the special signs may generally be reserved for friends.

In stating the rule I designedly used the words "ordinarily" and "generally" because exceptional circumstances may demand that even the special signs be shown to one's enemy or may, on the other hand, warrant at least the temporary withholding of the common signs. For example, to invite one to dinner is normally taken as a special sign of benevolence; yet, if John gives a party for "all the members of his class," he is not at liberty to exclude a classmate who is his enemy. He must, in this case, invite even the enemy, unless one of the excusing causes to be mentioned later is present. The same is to be said for Mary if she gives a dinner for "all the girls at the office," and for a religious who is in the habit of visiting "all who are in the infirmary." In such cases the special favors (inviting guests to dinner, visiting the sick) become to some extent common because they are extended to a certain group. If one's enemy belongs to this group, the common courtesy must be extended to him, too, unless special reasons, to be indicated later, excuse one from this obligation.

On some occasions, therefore, we must extend special favors even to our enemies. This is an exception to the general rule. On the other hand, the general rule that common signs must be shown the enemy also admits of exceptions. However, it is one thing to state that this rule admits of exceptions and quite another to formulate a reasonable policy that will govern the exceptional cases. I will give here some examples of cases (culled from various manuals of moral theology) in which the denial of these signs is considered reasonable, and after studying these examples we may be able to formulate a general principle that can be applied to all cases.

Everyone has a right to protect himself against mistreatment by others. Hence, in the event that a fellow religious is constantly indulging in a disagreeable form of teasing, ridicule, or rudeness, I may certainly defend myself by denying him ordinary courtesies until he mends his ways. For example, I might refuse to speak to him or to do a favor that I would ordinarily do for others, if such refusals were merely to show him that his conduct is painful and disagreeable and that I wish him to desist.

Superiors have the power within reasonable limits to punish their subjects. It is generally considered as within their punitive power to temporarily deny common courtesies to subjects who have given offense. Some authors think that in minor matters even equals may resort to this method of reasonably punishing another equal who has offended them. In other words, they consider that the hurt feeling that might be induced by temporary coldness and aloofness would be a just punishment for the offender and, therefore, a type of punishment that would be within the rights of private individuals.

Another reason that justifies a temporary exterior coldness towards an offender is the well-founded hope that such treatment will bring him to a better frame of mind. This is different from and in a higher order than mere punishment, even when justly inflicted.

There is also the problem of embarrassment. For a short time after a quarrel people usually feel extremely embarrassed in each other's presence. Avoidance of this mutual embarrassment would be a sufficient reason for temporarily keeping away from an enemy, even though that might mean the omission of one of the common signs of good will. For example, suppose that in a certain community it is customary for the religious to take turns visiting the sick during recreation. In this case, visiting the sick is a common sign of good will—that is, a kindness shown indiscriminately to all the members of the community who are ill. But suppose that two of the religious have recently quarreled, and one of them is now in the infirmary and it is the other's turn to visit him. It might be that consideration for the sick would excuse the second religious from making the visit. Of course, the ideal would be for both to forget it and for the visit to take place just as if there had been no quarrel; nevertheless, if the second religious honestly considered that the visit would be embarrassing and annoying to the sick person, he would be justified in omitting it.

Some people say that they avoid their enemy and do not speak to him or show him other signs of benevolence because they fear that this will lead to another quarrel, or that the enemy will put a sinister interpretation on their actions and use these as an occasion for offering further offense. Granted that the fear is well-founded, this is certainly a sufficient reason for omitting the customary expressions of good will. Of course, such fears are often groundless; but if one has really attempted to establish amicable relations with another and has met only with coldness or sharpness, there is certainly no obligation to continue the fruitless endeavor. In such a case the fault is all on one side.

Unfortunately, even in religion there are sour-minded individuals who refuse to get along with others, who cause great pain to fellow religious that wish to be courteous, and who, especially in a small house, are thorns in the side of the community. How they justify such conduct is somewhat of a mystery.

In the case just considered the obstacle to fraternal harmony was only one party. What of the case of two religious, members of the same community, who strongly dislike each other and either implicitly or explicitly agree to have nothing to do with each other? Are they justified by mutual agreement in failing to show to each other the common courtesies, such as speaking to each other?

To answer this question, I must separate the points that are clear from those that are not. The following points are clear: First, both religious are certainly obliged to abstain from what has previously been described as internal hatred. Secondly, each is obliged to be willing to extend to the other any spiritual or temporal help that might be of obligation according to the rules of well-ordered charity. Thirdly—and this is, it seems to me, all-important in community life—both are obliged to see that the community does not suffer because of their mutual estrangement policy. If they are members of a small community, it is practically impossible for them to carry out their program without causing much embarrassment and inconvenience to the other members of the community. Finally, both are obliged to see that their mutual coldness gives no scandal to externs. People naturally and justifiably expect to see religious live together in harmony and, if they notice a lack of harmony, their esteem of the religious life is considerably lowered.

Suppose that all the evils just mentioned could be avoided, would the mutual-estrangement policy still be sinful? The answer is not clear to me. However, even if such a situation is not sinful, it is at most "tolerable"—that is, it could be tolerated as a means of avoiding greater evils that might result from the mutual association of two immature characters. That the situation is not ideal, and that it is at variance with the spirit of Christ, seems quite clear. Moreover, the anomaly of the situation becomes even more glaring when one considers how often businessmen and businesswomen extend the most charming courtesy to those whom they dislike. This seems to be one case in which the children of this world are wiser

than the children of light: the former can do for
mere worldly gain what the latter will not do for the
love of Christ.

What has been said about mutual estrangement
among religious is equally applicable to similar situations among families or among other groups living
in common. And it should be remembered that the
smaller the group and the more closely the lives touch
one another, the more difficult it is to justify the
mutual-estrangement policy.

We are now in a position to sum up the doctrine
concerning the duty of showing the common signs of
benevolence. The ordinary rule is that these courtesies must be extended even to enemies because, being
common signs, they simply express externally our
recognition of a bond which unites the *group* and all
the members of the group. In other words, they are
extended to others as fellow men, fellow citizens, fellow religious, and so forth. To omit such courtesies
without good reason is usually a manifestation of ill
will or a lack of forgiveness, and even a sign of contempt; and because of these things, the omission of
the courtesies readily wounds the feelings of the enemy and is a source of scandal to others. However,
they may (and occasionally should) be omitted at
least for a time, to insure some greater good (such as
the correction of an offender and the safeguarding of
public discipline or private rights), and also to avoid
some greater evil (such as renewed quarreling).

Reconciliation

The duties thus far considered refer to an enemy
even in the wide sense: that is, to one who has given

no offense, but who is disliked. The duty of reconciliation supposes that there has been a quarrel; hence, the term "enemy" is here used in its strictest sense—namely, as "one who has given offense."

Each party to a quarrel is obliged to do his part to bring about a reconciliation. The offender (that is, the one who started the quarrel) must take the first step. As soon as he can reasonably do so, he must in some appropriate way express that he is sorry and that he is willing to make amends. A formal apology is not always necessary; in fact, it is frequently a source of embarrassment to both parties. It is often best to indicate in some indirect way that one is sorry. The offended party is obliged to accept the apology or its reasonable equivalent and to show that he has forgiven the offense and that he bears no ill will towards the offender.

Such are the basic duties of offender and offended. The following annotations may help to clarify them.

Some people say, "I forgive, but I cannot forget." Perhaps they mean that they have been so deeply wounded that the thoughts of the offense keep welling up in their mind and bring with them feelings of rancor. As I have already pointed out, such thoughts are no indication of sin, and therefore they do not indicate a lack of forgiveness. Sometimes, however, "I cannot forget" really means "I will not forget," and it indicates that there is still some deliberate ill will towards the offender.

Others say, "I don't wish ill to my offender, but I certainly can't wish him well." This, of course, is nonsense; for the well-wishing of true charity is deliberate supernatural love of the neighbor. Such well-wishing is not impossible for anyone, and anyone who is unwilling to cultivate this good will has not really forgiven his offender.

Forgiveness of an offense does not mean the waiving of the right to reparation for harm done. If an offense has harmed my reputation or caused me property loss, I am not unforgiving merely because I insist that the harm to reputation or property be repaired. Also, forgiveness is compatible with insistence on a just punishment for an offense; for even God inflicts punishments after having forgiven an offense. However, when human beings insist on punishment after expressing forgiveness, they must remember that they are not God and that their motives might be suspect. For instance, if a fellow religious offends me and then sincerely expresses his sorrow, and I still insist on revealing the matter to the superior so that my offender may be punished, it is quite likely that my forgiveness is not wholehearted.

The foregoing observations indicate, at least in a vague sort of way, what forgiveness is not. But what is it? Real forgiveness seems to reduce itself to this: a sincere willingness to restore the bond that existed before the quarrel, insofar as that is reasonably possible. Now, what if the bond was an intimate friendship? Moralists usually say that there is no strict obligation for the offended party to re-admit his offender to such intimacy. They say that since intimate friendship is something to which no one has a claim, the restoration of such friendship can hardly be urged as an obligation. The strict obligation, therefore, is usually satisfied when the offender is given those marks of charity that have previously been described as common.

The statement that forgiveness does not demand the re-establishment of an intimate friendship can be misleading. It seems to me that each case must be judged according to its own circumstances; and certainly there are occasions when the refusal to re-establish an intimate friendship after one quarrel (and perhaps a trifling one) is unreasonable, as well as unChristlike. However, if even a trifling quarrel is sufficient to undermine the confidence of the offended party in his offending friend, perhaps it is just as well that the friendship cease.

When should the first step towards reconciliation be taken? Moralists wisely suggest that it is generally expecting too much of an offended person to ask him to be reconciled immediately after a quarrel. He is entitled to a "cooling off" period. Normally, this need not be long; but the offender is justified in postponing his expression of sorrow until what seems to be an opportune time.

In many quarrels it is difficult to determine who was the first offender: both exploded more or less simultaneously. Theologians solve this problem by saying that the one who committed the more serious offense has the duty of taking the first step towards reconciliation. However, it must be admitted that this rule is also hard to apply because, at least in the eyes of the participants of the quarrel, the other party seems generally the more guilty.

As a matter of fact, daily experience shows us that no set of merely mechanical rules concerning the duties of offender and offended is perfectly satisfactory. The only really satisfactory solution to the difficulties that follow upon quarrels is that each party should be willing to take the initiative in reconciliation. After all, most of the difficulty for both parties is embarrassment. Frequently both want to make up, yet each is afraid to take the first step; and unfortunately this mutual embarrassment can lead to long and painful estrangements that could have been settled in a moment by a Christlike attitude and a sense of humor.

And I believe we can conclude this chapter on the same note. In the body of it, I have outlined the *duties* of loving the neighbor. It is well for everyone to know these and fulfill them; but it is also well to note that they represent a minimum. The Christian ideal, which is certainly the religious ideal, is to strive each day for perfect fulfillment of our Lord's words: "Love one another as I have loved you."

chapter 5

Detraction

"FATHER, can you give me a simple rule for determining when speech about others is sinful?"

The questioner I have in mind is not a religious of borderline ideals, not a religious with the how-far-can-I-go-without-sinning attitude. He is a religious who enjoys innocent recreation, a sincere religious with high ideals of justice and charity. But mixed with his idealism is a wholesome measure of realism. He knows that a resolve never to speak about personalities is rarely practicable; and he knows too that, other things being equal, it is more interesting to speak about personalities than about other topics. Intuitively he senses that not all conversation about the faults and foibles of others is sinful; yet, being a man of delicate conscience, he wants something more definite than his own intuition to enable him to recognize the borderline of sin and to keep his conversation far removed from it.

During many years of answering questions for religious, I have received numerous requests for articles giving the moral theology concerning unjust and unkind speech. In this chapter I am not attempting a complete expression of the moral theology on the subject; rather, I am presenting a selection of material with the definite purpose of formulating a set of safe, practical norms by which a religious may judge what is and what is not sinful in speech about others. It is hardly necessary to call attention to the fact that what is said here about speech applies also to other forms of communicating ideas—for example, letters.

For the most part, theologians treat of sinful speech about others under the head of detraction. The definitions of this sin vary somewhat; but I think that the essentials of all the definitions can be expressed as follows: *Detraction is the unjust blackening of an (absent) person's good name.* A few comments on this definition will take us into the heart of our subject.

Most people know what is meant by a good name, or a good reputation, although many may find difficulty in expressing their meaning in words. The theologian is not at a loss for words. He says that a person enjoys a good reputation when others think of him as possessing certain qualities for which people are wont to esteem one another. Primarily, these qualities pertain to the moral sphere: for example, we certainly esteem a person whom we think to be just, charitable, courageous, chaste, truthful, patient. However, virtue is not the only basis for a good reputation. Men are also held in high regard because they are good statesmen, good preachers, good teachers, good musicians, good writers, good disciplinarians, good companions, and so on. Likewise, they are respected for physical strength, for beauty (the moralists usually pause to indicate the women are particularly interested in this), and even for such purely external characteristics as nobility of birth, wealth, and prestige. In a word, a good reputation may be based on all qualities or accomplishments which good men look upon as worthy of esteem and praise.

The possession of a good reputation does not absolutely require that others think well of one. It is also possible to enjoy a good reputation in what I might call a purely negative sense, which consists in others' not thinking ill of one. For example, if a stranger moves into a neighborhood, his new neighbors may know nothing about him, either good or bad; yet it is clear that his reputation is really damaged if someone begins to spread word that he has just escaped from jail or been dismissed from his job because of cheating.

The word "blackening" was used in the definition of detraction by St. Albertus Magnus and St. Thomas Aquinas and has been repeated by most theologians who have written since their time. An expressive word, it is founded on the idea that a good reputations makes a man shine, or appear bright, in the minds of others, and that detraction either partially obscures or totally extinguishes this brightness.

St. Thomas enumerates several methods of blackening a name. The most obvious and least skillful of all is the unadorned lie, which consists in falsely attributing defects or faults to one's neighbor or in denying his good qualities. At the other end of the scale is unreserved truthfulness in revealing the neighbor's real, but hidden, faults. Between these two extremes of falsehood and truthfulness are several blackening methods which contain some falsity and some truth. For example, there is the method of exaggeration, which consists in making mountains out of molehills when discussing the neighbor's faults. Then there is the method of diminution—"damning with faint praise," as the saying goes. Many so-called good people are adept at this. They begin by recounting some praiseworthy achievement of their neighbor and, after they have thus won the confidence of their listeners, they proceed to show that what the neighbor did was no great accomplishment after all. More malicious perhaps than any of these methods is what is called the sinister interpretation, or the questioning of motives. Confronted with some evident good deed, the sinister-minded detractor will admit it but immediately add: "I wonder *why* he did that! I wonder what *he's* going to get out of it!"

A rather common trick of the detractor is what might be termed blackening by suggestion. Perhaps this is what St. Thomas meant by "malicious silence," or perhaps it may be reduced to exaggeration or diminution. At any rate, we are all familiar with it. The detractor starts to speak, and then stops with the heroic assertion, "Well, I guess I'd better not say it!" Or he may suggest, "Well, if I told the whole truth about this affair . . ." or "If you knew what really happened . . ." Statements like these leave the imagination free to rove over the whole campus of the seven deadly sins. They are devilishly effective in their blackening possibilities.

While I am on the subject of blackening, I might point out that not all recounting of the defects of others, even hitherto unknown defects, constitutes a blackening. All of us make mistakes or get ourselves into embarrassing situations which we personally find amusing and enjoy describing for the benefit of others. Such things do not lower us in the esteem of others, whether they are told by ourselves or our friends; hence they cannot ordinarily be material for detraction. It is not easy, however, to give an exact description of such things or to draw the line between them and incidents that might pertain to detraction. A similar situation is had with regard to teasing others. To some extent teasing can be quite wholesome. It makes for pleasant recreation and is an expression of the virtue that philosophers designate as *eutrapelia*. Yet, as it is very easy in speaking to another to cross the line from pleasant banter to ridicule, so in the matter of talking about others it is easy to go too far and tell things that are discrediting. Religious who keenly appreciate the feelings of others will readily recognize these borderlines and hardly need to make a special effort to avoid them. But religious who are overly devoted to their own sharp wit can well afford to err on the side of silence in such matters.

Many theologians put the word "absent" in their definitions of detraction. St. Thomas does this equivalently when he defines detraction as the blackening of another person's reputation by "secret" words—that is, by words spoken behind one's back. In English we sometimes refer to this by the very significant word "backbiting." This notion of absence, or be-hind-the-back, is put into the definition of detraction to distinguish it from the sin of contumely, which is usually committed by speaking offensively to another. However, absence, if taken literally, is not essential to detraction, for it can happen that by one and the same act one commits both detraction and contumely: for example, by unjustly charging a man with certain faults to his face and in the presence of others. In this way the man himself is personally insulted and his reputation is also injured in the minds of the others who are present.

"Unjust" is the last word in the definition that calls for comment. Detraction, understood in its technical sense, is a sin of injustice, like theft or murder. Theft violates a man's right to his property; murder violates his right to life; and detraction violates his right to a good reputation. Detraction, therefore, is not just an unkindness; it is more than that. It is the damaging or destruction of something very precious which belongs to another. Of course, like theft, detraction can be, and often is, a venial sin; but even when only small, it is a little worse than a "small unkindness."

In general, there are two reasons why a man might possess a good reputation: namely, he is either *actually* good or *apparently* good. If he is actually good—that is, if he really possesses the good qualities people think he possesses—then his right to his reputation is absolute. No one could take it from him without sinning, because it could be taken away only by lying. Even when only apparently good—that is, when he really is not what people think him to be—he retains some right to his reputation, since the common good and his own social nature call for some restrictions with regard to the revelation of his hidden defects. But in this case his right to his good name is limited by many factors; and those who know his secret faults are sometimes justified, or even obliged, to manifest them to others, even though this manifestation will diminish or even destroy his good reputation.

What reasons justify the revelation of another's secret faults? Before I answer this question I should like to make it clear that I am not referring here to cases in which the person who knows the secret faults of another has acquired this knowledge in any confidential capacity—as spiritual director, say, or as superior, as student counselor, and of course as a confessor. In other words, I am not speaking of the revelation of an entrusted secret. That is a special subject. The knowledge thus acquired is governed by special norms, and it would simply complicate our present subject to treat it here.

Understanding, therefore, that we are not speaking of the entrusted secret, I can best indicate the reasons which allow us and sometimes oblige us to reveal the hidden faults of others by a simple example. Suppose James, who is generally thought to be a most upright boy, is in reality a thief; and suppose John knows it. John might reveal the fact to the school authorities so that the rest of the school could be protected against James; and this would be for the common good. Or John might speak of James's fault to a friendly priest for the purpose of correcting James; and this would be for James's own good. Or John might give this information to a friend who was about to hire James; and this would be for the good of his friend, an innocent third party. Or, finally, John might reveal James's fault in order to protect himself from injury by James.

The example sufficiently indicates the four reasons that permit, and sometimes demand, the revelation of someone's secret defects: the common good, the greater good of the person having the defects, the good of an innocent third party, and the good of the party who reveals the defect. Theologians give many examples of cases in which one or more of these reasons might be verified. Some of these examples are of considerable pertinence to religious, and it will be useful to cite them here.

It is for the common good in religious communities to reveal to those concerned the probably harmful defects of those who are being considered for election or appointment to office. It is likewise for the common good to reveal abuses to canonical visitors. And, as the case may be, it is for the common good or the good of an innocent third party to make known to proper authorities the misconduct of a religious that is likely to injure the community or that is actually harming another religious or even a pupil. It is for the good of one's own soul to speak to the superior about what one finds an occasion of sin, even though this may reflect on someone else. And it may be for the good of the culprit to speak to the superior for the sincere purpose of helping him to amend. Of course, religious who are too prone to see faults and abuses and to cry wolf can readily go too far in these matters; but, on the other hand, it is amazing to see how some religious can neglect a serious obligation towards their own community, and even to the whole Church, because of an entirely false loyalty to a friend or because they adhere blindly to a sort of American-Boy code of "not squealing."

Authors generally say that if one has suffered some secret injustice or unkindness at the hands of another, one may reveal this to a single prudent person for the sake of obtaining consolation or advice. The supposition here is that the one prudent person will keep the information to himself and that the name of the offender will not be divulged unless it is necessary for accomplishing these purposes. A confessor would certainly be considered a prudent person who would keep the information to himself. Moreover, one can usually unburden oneself in confession and obtain advice without giving any clue to the identity of the offender.

The foregoing are some of the reasons why religious may, and sometimes should, reveal the secret faults of others. In such cases they do no injustice, even though someone's good name is hurt, because the right to one's good name is limited and does not extend to these cases. Hence, there is no detraction when secret faults are revealed for a sufficient reason.

It should be clear that there can be no question of detraction in the strict sense—that is, of an injustice —in speaking of a person's faults or defects with someone who already knows them or in circumstances in which the knowledge of these faults or defects has become, so to speak, public property. However, it is not always easy to determine when and to what extent such knowledge may be considered public property. Theologians go to great lengths to explain "publicity," and I could use some perfectly good space here in trying to explain their explanations. But that does not interest me right now. At present I prefer to point out something which seems to be of greater significance for our purpose: namely, that even when a man has lost the right to his reputation by the fact that the knowledge of his defects has become public property, it is not necessarily true that speaking about these defects is *sinless*. The mutual relationships of human beings, after all, are governed not only by justice but also by charity; and charity may continue to impose a duty even when the claims of strict justice are non-existent.

Let me illustrate what I mean by an example taken from the writings of an eminent modern moralist. A certain man has committed a crime for which he has been justly sentenced to serve a term in prison. All theologians agree that a juridical sentence like that would deprive a man of all *right* to keep the knowledge of this crime secret. In other words, anyone could speak of his crime, even to one who had not heard of it, without violating strict justice. Furthermore, it seems rather commonly agreed that this privation of right is perpetual and that the man will never again have a strict right to silence concerning his misdeed. This man, who has thus lost his right to a good name, serves his prison sentence, returns to

[116]

the world, and goes to a place where he is not known to begin life anew. He is honestly trying to make a new start and is succeeding. He is harming no one and is a menace to no one. Then one day someone who knows of his former misconduct comes upon the scene, makes known the criminal offense, casts suspicion upon the ex-criminal, and finally ruins him. It is obvious that, even though the informer in this case did not violate strict justice (something which is not too clear, despite the opinions of great theologians), he has certainly failed to keep the law "Thou shalt love thy neighbor as thyself." Without any objectively solid reason for doing so, he has brought harm and suffering to a fellow human being.

I have introduced this instance of a violation of charity because I believe that any discussion of detraction—which concerns only injustice—tends to be unsatisfactory and to create a wrong impression unless something is added concerning the law of charity which must be observed in speaking about the faults of others. This duty of charity may be stated as follows: *Even when strict justice is not violated by speaking about the faults of others, charity, nevertheless, obliges one to say nothing which will unnecessarily cause harm or sorrow to one's neighbor.*

Those who have had sufficient patience, or at least sufficient curiosity, to read up to this point are no doubt wondering when I shall try to answer the question with which I introduced this chapter. I think we have had sufficient general discussion to begin to come to grips with the question, but I am not ready even yet to try to formulate a single, simple rule for determii..ng what is sinful speech about others. Rather, I should like to point out what seem to be all the ordinary ways in which religious might sin, either against charity or against justice, in their speech about others. As I see it, among all matters treated in the theological discussions of detraction and uncharitable speech, the following ways of sinning are worthy of special consideration by religious:

(1) *Calumny.*—Calumny consists in representing another person as worse than he really is. As I mentioned when discussing the various methods of blackening one's reputation, this may be accomplished either by the unadorned lie or by some more subtle form of misrepresentation, like making light of his merits, exaggerating his faults, casting undue suspicion on his motives, or suggesting things that are not true. Religious may seldom have recourse to a bald lie about another, but they can well examine themselves and beware of these other forms of misrepresentation.

(2) *The unjustifiable revelation of true, but secret, faults.*—Despite the fact that we lead a community life and that our actions are generally easily observed by the community, most of us have some faults or perform some misdeeds that are known only to a few others These are termed secret faults, and they may not be revealed even to other members of the same community without a sufficient reason. I have already indicated some reasons which might make such a revelation justifiable. To reveal discrediting things without one of those reasons is an injustice.

(3) *The unjustifiable revelation to externs of the faults of a member of the community which may be known within the community itself, but not outside.* —An extern is anyone who does not belong to the same religious institute. The word refers, therefore, to members of other religious institutes, to diocesan priests, to students in our schools, nurses in our hospitals, and so forth.

Here I should note a profound difference between a religious community and what may be called a civic community, such as a village, a town, a city. The civic community is termed "open." Of its very nature it has free communication with other such communities. The ordinary teaching of theologians is that if a man's faults are well-known, or public, in one open community, they may be recounted without injustice in other open communities. This applies to communications made by word of mouth, by letter, by newspaper, or other similar means.

A religious community, on the contrary, is like a family and is called a "closed" community. Of its very nature it preserves secrets from the rest of the world. Hence, all theologians agree that even when faults or misdeeds of a religious are well-known to all the members of his own community, he still retains a strict right to keep this knowledge from externs. The unjustifiable recounting of such things to an extern is an injustice to the individual about whom the revelation is made; and, besides this, it may easily result in a discrediting of the religious community itself. I hardly need dwell on the harm such rash speech can do to potential vocations.

Only in very rare cases is there a sufficient reason for revealing these faults to externs. As I have already pointed out, a religious who is in need of counsel may consult a confessor, even though this might mean the revelation of some abuses in the community. A religious may and should manifest abuses to a canonical visitor. Also, a religious may certainly take advantage of the right of appeal which is allowed by the Church, even though this entails the revelation to some higher ecclesiastical authority of real or apparent injustices inflicted by a superior. In a certain sense, however, these revelations to canonical visitors and to higher authorities are not revelations made to externs, since insofar as these ecclesiastics exercise authority over the institute, they may be said to belong to it.

(4) *The unjustifiable revelation to members of another house of the same institute of faults well-known only in the religious' own house.*—I think I may safely say theologians generally agree that this peddling of discrediting stories from one religious house to another is wrong; but in many cases it is not clear to me whether they consider it an injustice or merely a violation of charity. It seems to me that the religious ordinarily has a strict right to keep the knowledge of his misdeeds within the confines of his own house and that this type of inter-house gossip is an injustice. However, since the general teaching seems obscure on this point, I would give as a practical rule that such inter-house gossip is certainly a violation of the law of charity, but not clearly an injustice.

(5) *The unjustifiable recalling of defects that were once well-known, but which have since been forgotten because the culprit has reformed.*—Earlier in these notes I indicated a case in which a person lost the right to his reputation because he was justly sentenced by a judge. It seems that when one loses his right in that particular manner (namely, by a juridical sentence) the loss is perpetual, and that the subsequent recalling of his crime would not be an injustice—though, as I indicated, it could be a violation of charity.

It would hardly be practical to discuss the juridical loss of reputation here, because it would seldom have any application to religious. A religious, however, might more readily earn an unsavory reputation in his own community by reason of his open misconduct; and of course, as long as that misconduct is open and well-known, he cannot be said to have a right to have his faults kept secret in the community in which he lives. But it often happens that a religious who is a "Peck's bad boy" at one period of his religious life later reforms. His old faults are forgotten and his good name is regained. Just as he lost his right through his own misconduct, so he has recovered it through his own good conduct; and anyone who insists on revealing his old Adam in a discrediting way is, according to most theologians, violating justice. Some people have most exasperating memories in this regard. We may have been unbearable community nuisances in our younger days, and we may regret it exceedingly and thank God that it is all forgotten, when lo! one of these people with the provocative memories will pop up with, "Well, he's all right now, but you should have known him when. . . ." Of course, some of these stories are told with the best of intentions, to show what grand progress we have made; and they may actually do us good, not harm. Nevertheless, this recalling of the bad old days is a dangerous pastime; and it is much better to leave it to the recording angel on Judgment Day.

(6) *Preventing a person from regaining his good name by uselessly reminding others of his faults.*— This is slightly different from the preceding case. There, the religious had already regained his good name; here, his misconduct is recent and still well-known in his community. While this condition lasts it is not an injustice for the other members of that community to speak of his faults among themselves. Nevertheless, in the ordinary course of events, people do forget things, even our faults, if they are not perpetually reminded of them. And—also in the ordinary course of events—it is to be presumed that any religious, save an utterly hopeless case, would like to reform and to regain esteem in the minds of his fellow religious. Charity demands that he be given a reasonable opportunity.

(7) *Recreational gossip among members of the community about the well-known faults of an absent member, unless such gossip is utterly harmless and could not be reasonably resented by the absent member if he knew about it.*—For the proper understanding of this case—and perhaps for the preceding cases, too—I wish to recall something to which I referred earlier in these notes. I mentioned that all of us have

characteristics ("idiosyncrasies," if you wish to use the term) or do absurd things which we do not mind speaking about at recreation and do not resent having others describe. Granted the proper spirit of moderation and delicate respect for the feelings of others, these things are legitimate subjects of conversation. They do not lower anyone in the esteem of others, and speaking about them would be resented only by the extraordinarily sensitive.

What are those characteristics and foibles, the discussion of which is quite harmless? It is hard to give an exact definition or description of them. One learns them through experience. Here are a few examples: one person is absent-minded; a professor has certain mannerisms; another person has the habit of using the wrong words; someone has an embarrassing experience with a superior; or the naïve question of a student puts one on the spot.

This seventh rule really comes to this: in speaking about the faults or foibles of others at recreation, one should faithfully adhere to the golden rule. In other words, put yourself in the other person's place, and if you judge that, in his place, you would reasonably object to what you are about to say, *do not say it.* The violation of this rule in the circumstances given here (namely, by recreational gossip about the well-known faults of others) is an offense against charity.

Those who are normally sensitive should be able to apply the golden rule very easily, but an extraordinarily callous person may not use his own disposition as a norm for judging the reasonable reactions of others. The point to be emphasized about the golden rule when applied to conversation is that the speaker should put himself *in the other person's place.*

But even this putting of oneself in another person's place has certain limits when there is question of strict obligation. For instance, if the other person is extraordinarily sensitive and would resent a story or a remark merely because of his exaggerated sensitiveness, it is hardly fair to make this a basis of strict obligation for a whole community. Resentment that springs only from extraordinary sensitiveness need not be considered as reasonable resentment. Hence, there appears to be no strict obligation to guard against it in conversation. However, I believe it is a fine *ascetical* rule to have regard even for these cases. One certainly cannot go wrong if one's constant policy is to avoid anything that would be uselessly offensive even to the hypersensitive.

Speaking of hypersensitivity reminds me of another point which is of some importance in the application of the golden rule. I mean that in judging reactions according to this rule we must to some extent have regard for *individual* differences. Suppose we consider a group of ten people, all of whom might be described as normally sensitive. Very likely each one of these ten is extremely touchy about some one thing. For example, one young woman might thoroughly enjoy all the jokes her friends tell about her, except jokes concerning her cooking. A priest may have no objection to any stories told about his characteristic oddities, except when they concern his manner of saying Mass.

These are but examples. The idea I wish to bring out is that in gaging the reasonable resentment of others one cannot simply say: "I don't mind what people say about my cooking, therefore she shouldn't mind, either." We have to keep in mind that even normal people differ, and that these individual differences do not indicate hypersensitivity. The hypersensitive person is usually sensitive about many things; that is why it is extremely difficult to avoid saying things that would offend him.

(8) *Encouraging others to carry on unjust or uncharitable conversation.*—Thus far I have indicated what seem to me the ordinary ways a religious might violate justice or charity in his own speech about others. The seventh rule put the finishing touch on all the others, and the present one may seem like an anticlimax. However, one can hardly bring up the subject of speech about others without saying something on the morality of *listening*. Now, I think that, practically speaking, the only usual way of sinning by listening is to prompt or encourage others to indulge in detraction or uncharitable speech.

Theoretically, of course, the listener may sin internally by approving of the sinful speech of others or by fostering hatred for the one being detracted. Theoretically, also, one may sin by not stopping detraction or unkind speech when one can conveniently do so. But, since I am listing the ordinary ways of sinning, I think that these two sources of sin can be ignored. Insistence on the idea of sinning by "internal approving or rejoicing" simply generates scruples. There are very few people, religious included, who can effectively put a stop to a "poison" party; hence, I think it quite safe to say that ordinarily those who merely listen without giving encouragement do not sin. Whether or not it is advisable to try to change the subject or to politely excuse oneself will depend on circumstances. If maneuvers like these are not accomplished with great tact, they do more harm than good.

Someone might ask, "But what constitutes *encouragement?*" I can attempt an indirect answer to this question by citing a case from one of the standard moral theology case books (books of moral problems that illustrate the principles given in the manuals).

Father Genicot, the author of this particular book, tells the fictitious story of a certain Barbara, a good Catholic woman who runs an old-fashioned store. Dealings were rather informal in these stores, which readily became centers for the town gossip. And Barbara, who is not given to gossip, encounters this problem. Occasionally she cannot avoid listening to her customers while they indulge in the systematic ripping of characters. Barbara lets them talk, and now and then, just to avoid being considered an absolute dummy, puts in a remark like "My goodness, who'd have thought such a nice girl would do that!" or "Dear me, I wonder why I never heard that before."

The student's problem is to decide whether Barbara's conduct encourages the others to keep up their detracting. The obvious answer is that it does not. But the case would be quite different if, at the first indication of the ripping ceremony, Barbara would put aside her work, thrust her chin over the counter and, eyes bright with eagerness, say: "Um-m, tell me all about it." That would be encouragement. And I don't know any other way of indicating the difference between merely tolerant listening to detraction and genuine willing encouragement.

I have wandered through so many paragraphs since putting the introductory question that perhaps I should repeat it. "Father, can you give me a simple rule for determining when speech about others is sinful?" The simplest answer I know is the following: "Speech about others is sinful when it violates the golden rule; that is, when either your own speech or your encouragement of others' could be reasonably resented by the person being talked about." Properly understood, this single rule covers everything, from serious injustice to slight violations of charity; but I think that the other rules and the lengthy explanations were necessary for a proper understanding of it.

PART III

The Sacraments

The heading of this section may perhaps be misleading, because certainly these few chapters do not say all that should be said about the use of the sacraments as means of sanctification in the religious life. Rather, these chapters simply concentrate on a few basic notions that must be well understood if religious are to make proper use of the many suggestions ascetical manuals make concerning the sacraments.

Each of the chapters deals with what I have found to be a genuine practical problem in the lives of religious. One problem arises from a certain mental confusion over what is required for the fruitfulness of a devotional confession. Another concerns ways of increasing the efficacy of the sacrament of penance, even independently of any help offered by the confessor. These problems are treated in the first two chapters. Since the first chapter is general, and the second a development of a particular point, there is necessarily some repetition; but I think the repetition should be helpful.

The third chapter deals with a problem that is of special, though by no means exclusive, pertinence to religious women: namely, the wise use of the various privileges the Church now officially grants to religious regarding the choice of a confessor. Finally, there is the matter of the dispositions required for, as well as the abuses that might accompany, the practice of frequent Communion. The Holy See has manifested a deep concern that religious be well acquainted with the legislation regarding frequent Communion, not only for their own personal sanctification, but also for the proper training of the youth committed to their charge. The last chapter of this section explains one of the most important aspects of that legislation.

chapter 6

Good Confessions and Better Confessions

RELIGIOUS not infrequently experience a vague sense of dissatisfaction with their confessions. They must confess weekly, generally at a certain time, even though they are not in the mood. At times they must make a rather hasty immediate preparation for confession. Their sins are usually "small sins"; in fact, it is often difficult to focus on any really definite sins to confess. A certain amount of routine seems unavoidable, though routine confessions are strongly condemned by many spiritual writers. Finally, most religious have read or heard of the many advantages of frequent devotional confession, and they want to reap some of these fruits for themselves. Yet, despite their holy desires, they are even inclined to wonder whether their confessions are not entirely fruitless.

Very likely there is no absolute remedy for a sense of dissatisfaction in those who are striving for perfection. Some dissatisfaction is natural, even helpful. But this holy sense of dissatisfaction is different from discouragement, worry, or a vague feeling of uneasiness. As much as possible, the dissatisfaction should be clearly defined, because only then can it be used constructively as a steppingstone to the attainment of one's ideals.

My purpose in the present chapter is to propose a few rules that may help religious clarify any dissatisfaction they may feel with their confessions and give some definite direction to their efforts at self-improvement. The rules enunciate nothing new. No doubt most religious know them well; yet I believe that some fail to apply them and, consequently, are conscious of a waste of effort, a lack of perfect peace of mind, and sometimes discouragement. If all religious, from the novitiate onward, would observe these rules faithfully, they would be much more satisfied with their confessions and would reap many definite advantages from them.

Four Rules

In formulating these rules, and in commenting on them, I am limiting the subject to the devotional confession, as this is the type that religious most frequently make.[1] Keeping this in mind—namely, that we are speaking only of the devotional confession— we may state the rules as follows:

Rule 1: Be sure to confess, at least in a general way, some real, subjective sin that you have certainly committed.

[1] By a devotional confession is meant a confession in which there is no *necessary* matter for confession. Necessary matter means mortal sins committed after baptism and not yet directly absolved. A confession may still be devotional in the theological sense, even though it is prescribed by rule.

[132]

Rule 2: Have genuine, supernatural contrition, at least imperfect, for some sin included in your confession.

Rule 3: Be willing to accept and to perform any justly imposed penance.

Rule 4: Try to sanctify yourself through confession by cultivating a more effective purpose of amendment.

It may be well to call attention immediately to the decided difference between the first three rules and the fourth rule. The first three express *minimum essentials*; the fourth expresses an *ideal*. A penitent who observes the first three rules makes a *good* confession; a penitent who keeps not only the first three, but also the fourth, makes a *better* confession. This is an important distinction. Our ideal, of course, is to make the *better* confession; but there is a great deal of consolation and peace of mind in knowing that our confessions are *good,* even though they could be better. A good confession of devotion always produces some grace in the soul.

Good Confessions

It would be a wise policy for every religious to have a twofold aim in making his confessions: first, to make a *good* confession by fulfilling all minimum essentials; and, secondly, to make his confession even *better* by the use of some practicable plan for applying the fourth rule. In keeping with this twofold aim, I am dividing the remainder of this chapter into two parts, which treat respectively of a *good* confession and a *better* confession.

Confession of Sins

On the part of the penitent, three things are required for the reception of the sacrament of penance: confession of sins, contrition, and satisfaction. The first rule enunciates the minimum essentials for the first of these acts. It is certainly not difficult for anyone to fulfill this rule in a devotional confession. It is sufficient to confess any or all of the venial sins committed since the last confession, or any mortal sin or venial sin of one's past life (provided it was committed after baptism). A penitent can even fulfill this rule by always confessing the same sin from his past life. He once culpably missed Mass on Sunday, let us say, and since then, in his devotional confessions, he never mentions anything specifically but that one sin. "There's nothing special since my last confession, Father," he says week after week, "but in my past life I once missed Mass through my own fault." Finally, the penitent does not have to do even as much as that in a devotional confession. It suffices if he simply includes his sins in a general way: for example, "There's nothing special since my last confession, but I want to include all the sins of my life."

The repetition, week after week, of the same sin from the past, without confessing any new matter, is not, of course, the ideal. Nor is the ideal to make a merely general accusation. Yet such accusations are, strictly speaking, sufficient in a devotional confession, provided the penitent has the requisite contrition—as will be explained in the comments on the second rule.[2] I have referred to such accusations, not to encourage their use, but simply to indicate how easy it is to live up to the demands of the first rule.

Despite the fact that it is comparatively easy to observe the first rule, it is also possible for well-meaning penitents—even religious—to violate it and to make unintentionally fruitless [3] confessions. Perhaps a few sample confessions—entirely fictitious, of course—will serve to illustrate what I mean.

A religious is preparing for confession. To him, as he examines his conscience, the past week looks black enough. On Sunday, when he assisted at Mass he certainly did everything that the Church requires for the complete fulfillment of the obligation; yet he was no seraph at Mass: he could surely have assisted more devoutly. On Monday he felt a strong inspiration of grace to pass up the butter at one meal; and on Tuesday he felt an equally strong inspiration of grace to spend a half-hour of his free time before the Blessed Sacrament. He neglected both these divine invitations. Finally, despite the fact that his rule or-

[2] The unnecessary use of the merely generic accusation, without mentioning anything in particular (e.g., "There's nothing special since my last confession, Father; but I want to include in this confession all the sins of my life"), is particularly to be discouraged. By reason of a more or less general custom in the Church, penitents who make devotional confessions are expected to mention some particular kind of sin, either from their past life or committed since their last confession.

[3] For the benefit of students of theology who might read this article, let me say that in speaking of the confession of devotion I use the words "fruitless" and "invalid" indiscriminately. The valid devotional confession must, I believe, be fruitful.

dered that all should make their beds before the morning meditation, he three times put off this distasteful task until after breakfast. Of course, his institute states explicitly that merely disciplinary rules, not involving the vows, do not bind under pain of sin; but this, he tells himself, is no excuse for him. He enters the confessional and accuses himself as follows: "Since my last confession I was negligent in my prayers; I was ungrateful to God; and I was disobedient. That's all I can remember, Father."

Another religious, in preparing for confession, notes that he has often felt strong resentment against someone who offended him, that he has had many distractions during meditation, and that on one occasion he made a remark that hurt someone's feelings. He might note also that the feelings and distractions were not voluntary and that the offending remark was unintentional; yet these excuses do not occur to him. He confesses as follows: "Since my last confession I was uncharitable in thought and speech and was distracted in my prayers. That'll be all, Father."

A third religious has had a really trying time of it since his last confession. He has been literally besieged by a strong temptation to impurity of thought; in fact, the temptation has been so strong that he really does not know how he stands before God. He decides to go to confession "just to be safe." In confession he says: "I had a very strong temptation against purity, and I want to accuse myself insofar as I am guilty before God. There's nothing else bothering me, Father."

I have chosen these three fictitious confessions because they illustrate defects which, though very likely uncommon, could make a confession unintentionally fruitless. In the first confession, only imperfections, not *real* sins, were confessed. In the second, the things mentioned might have been sins, but there was no *subjective* guilt: the uncharitable feelings and distracting thoughts were involuntary, the offending remark was unintentional. In the third, there was no *certain* matter: the penitent may have been guilty of mortal or venial sin, but he may have committed no sin at all.

All of these confessions are at least probably defective. Yet all could be saved from fruitlessness by the intelligent use of a concluding accusation such as "I include in this confession all the sins of my life"; "I want to include all the sins of my past life"; or "For these, and for all the sins of my life, especially for . . . , I ask pardon from almighty God and penance and absolution from you, Father." It is true that accusations like these can become purely mechanical and practically meaningless, yet they are infinitely better than conclusions like "That's all I remember"—which adds nothing to the confession, or "That'll be all"—which sounds like a person buying groceries. It is hardly advisable to force religious to make subtle distinctions between imperfections and venial sins; but it surely is advisable for all penitents who habitually commit only small sins to have some concluding accusation which covers up a possible insufficiency of matter in their confessions.

As I said, these confessions are purely fictitious. If they occurred in real life, a confessor would generally note the deficiency and ask a question or two that would save them from invalidity. This might not always be done, however, and penitents should be trained to make good confessions independently of questions by the confessor.

Contrition

The second rule gives the minimum essential for contrition in the devotional confession. Here again, it is important to distinguish between the ideal and the essential. Of all the acts of the penitent, contrition is the most important; and everyone's ideal should be to have a profound and effective contrition. Yet the confession can be good, even though contrition be far from the ideal. The ideal, even in a devotional confession, is perfect contrition, though imperfect suffices. The ideal is that the contrition extend to all sins confessed, though it is enough if at applies to any sin included in the confession.[4] The ideal is that contrition be deeply moving, like Magdalen's; though it is sufficient if the contrition be as unemotional as paying the rent.

Important as it is, it is not extremely difficult to have sufficient contrition for a fruitful devotional

---

[4] When I say that it is sufficient if the contrition applies to only one of the sins confessed, I mean that it is enough for the absolution and the reception of grace through the sacrament. This does not mean that all the other venial sins are forgiven. Sins for which there is no repentance at all are not forgiven either in confession or outside of confession. For example, a penitent who has committed two venial sins and has true sorrow for one but *no* sorrow for the other, would receive grace through the sacrament but not forgiveness for the one unrepented sin. His confession would be fruitful, but it could be more fruitful.

confession. A penitent who has once committed a mortal sin and repented of it, and now includes that sin in his confession, either mentioning it by name or including it in a general accusation, may take it for granted that he has sufficient contrition if he continues in his good resolve to avoid all mortal sin. A penitent who has committed a deliberate venial sin in the past and now includes it in his confession, either specifically or at least in his general accusation, has sufficient contrition if he renews his good resolve to avoid that sin in future. Even a penitent who includes only the "smaller" venial sins in his confession—the semi-deliberate sins, as they are sometimes called—has sufficient contrition if he is sincerely resolved to try to do better in *some* way (for example, by eliminating one kind of sin or a certain class of sins, or even by reducing the number of his small sins).

We generally speak of contrition for sin as if it were one simple act. In reality it seems to involve a rather complicated process. It would not be worth our while to go deeply into this process now; but it may be useful to indicate here that, in making an act of contrition, a penitent should pay particular attention to two elements of the psychological process: namely, motivation and purpose of amendment. If these two elements are present, one may safely assume that an act of contrition is good; if either one is lacking, there is no real contrition.

Motivation is not contrition, but is a necessary prelude to it. The sinner must realize the evil of his acts before he can truly repent of them. And he must see this evil through the eyes of faith if his contrition, whether in or out of confession, is to be supernatural and effective.

As we know, faith supplies us with a variety of motives for repentance, some more perfect than others. It shows us sin as contrary to the will of God and therefore as something against God's infinite holiness and goodness; it shows us the Son of God suffering on the Cross for our sins; it reveals sin as ingratitude to God, our supreme benefactor; it tells us of the richness of heaven, of the terrible fate of hell, of the punishments of purgatory, and of the temporal punishments for sin in this life.

All penitents should keep in mind that the motive for their contrition should be applicable to the sins for which they wish to be sorry. In particular, it is necessary for those who want to make an act of contrition for venial sins to remember that not all motives that apply to mortal sins are applicable to venial sins. Despite the fact that many books speak of venial sins in the most thunderous terms, venial sin is *not* mortal sin. Mortal sin destroys the likeness of God in the soul; venial sin does not. Mortal sin breaks the bond of friendship between the soul and God; venial sin does not. Mortal sin is deserving of hell; venial sin is not.

In recalling these differences I am not trying to minimize venial sins. I simply insist on the necessity of seeing them in their true perspective in order to elicit a genuine act of contrition for them. The motive of fear of hell applies to contrition for venial sins only in a roundabout way—because, for example, venial sins may lead to mortal sin, which is deserving of hell. On the other hand, there are many other motives which apply directly to venial sins, even to the smallest of them. Venial sins are contrary to God's holy will; they defeat His wise plans for our sanctification and for our attainment of a certain degree of heavenly glory; they manifest a failure to appreciate His gifts; they are a shabby return for what our Lord did for us; they are deserving of some punishment in this life or in purgatory. It would be well for those who make devotional confessions to meditate occasionally, especially during the time of retreat, on motives such as these so that they may briefly and intelligently recall appropriate motives when preparing for confession.

From the point of view of motivation, therefore, it is perhaps easier to make an act of contrition for mortal sin than it is for venial sin. At least it is easier to see the evil of mortal sin.

As for the purpose of amendment, less is required for venial sin than for mortal sin. No matter what mortal sins a penitent has committed, he has not sufficient contrition unless his purpose of amendment extends to all mortal sins. He must will to avoid all of them in the future. Thus, the ordinary definition of a purpose of amendment as "a firm purpose to sin no more" applies quite literally to mortal sins. But this does not seem to be strictly necessary with regard to venial sins. In fact, with regard to all the smaller sins taken together, it is hardly possible. Rather, in the case of sorrow for venial sins, the essential thing is the *sincere will to do better*.

This distinction between mortal and venial sins, with respect to purpose of amendment, is based on the fundamental difference between these two kinds of sin. Mortal sin, of its nature, implies a rejection of God's friendship; hence, one cannot will to gain or continue in God's friendship unless he intends to try to avoid all mortal sin, without exception. But one who commits only venial sins is already a friend of God, and this friendship admits of many degrees and of continuous growth. There is no contradiction in willing to avoid some venial sins but not others, or in willing to reduce the total number of one's venial sins without proposing to avoid venial sin entirely.

Satisfaction

The third rule enunciates the minimum essential for the third act of the penitent—satisfaction. I stated it merely for the sake of completeness. The rule itself hardly requires comment or explanation, except perhaps to remark—what is probably obvious—that there is a difference between willingness to accept a penance and the actual performance of the penance. The willingness is required for the validity of the confession; without this disposition a confession would not be good. The actual performance of the penance, however, does not pertain to the essence of the sacrament but only to its completion and perfection.

Better Confessions

The first three rules, as I said, express the minimum essentials of a fruitful confession. All who make

[142]

a devotional confession, even religious, should have as their first aim to keep those rules. But religious, in particular, should not be content with that. Their aim should be to make their confessions *better,* especially through the observance of the fourth rule.

Many books and articles offer suggestions for improving our confessions. Here I should like to suggest merely one workable plan for using confession as an instrument of self-improvement in the way of perfection; and I think I can accomplish my purpose better by an example than by a long discussion.

A religious is making his annual retreat. In surveying the past year he notices that he has committed many small sins. He wants to correct them and, in particular, two habitual faults: uncharitable speech and small sins against poverty. He determines what means he will take to avoid these faults and makes his resolutions accordingly. When his program is all prepared, he suddenly realizes, with a twinge of conscience, that he has made similar resolutions in previous retreats and that in a very short time they were either badly mutilated or completely ignored. He knows he had a sincere purpose of amendment; what he lacked was something to sustain that purpose of amendment through the year following the retreat.

Confronted with the vexing problem of an unsustained purpose of amendment, the religious decides to solve it by effecting a link between his retreat resolutions and his weekly confessions in the coming year.

The retreat ends and the days go by till it is time for the weekly confession. In examining his conscience, the religious looks first to his retreat resolutions. He has kept them this week. He thanks God, renews his good resolution and, having finished his examination of conscience, he confesses as follows: "Since my last confession I have . . . . I accuse myself of these and of all the other sins of my life, especially uncharitable speech and sins against poverty."

Another week goes by, with the same results. The examination of conscience and the accusation of the two special kinds of sin are made in the same way. In the third week, there is a slight falling off. Before confession the religious recalls the motives for avoiding these sins, asks pardon for his falls, and renews his good resolution. In confession he accuses himself as follows: "Since my last confession I was uncharitable in speech twice and committed one small sin against poverty. In my annual retreat I determined to correct these faults, and I want to ask pardon for them now and to renew my purpose of amendment. I include in this confession all the sins of my life."

Enough for the example. In giving it I do not mean that everything must be taken literally. Ten penitents might follow the same general plan, yet use ten slightly different methods in applying it. The important thing is the general plan—the linking of the retreat resolutions with the subsequent confessions.

The plan that I have suggested may not be suitable to all; but, in the absence of a better one, it is worth trying. It offers definite help along the lines of motivation and of concentrated effort at amendment of faults. Retreat is a time of great grace; seldom will our motivation be nobler or more clearly perceived, and any plan which will help to recall that motivation must be profitable. I think it is a truism that in the spiritual life, whether on the negative or the positive side, there must be some concentration of effort. We cannot rid ourselves of all faults at once; we cannot acquire all virtues at once.

I realize that this plan involves some monotony, but I do not know of any plan for spiritual progress that does not. If more variety is really required, the objectives can be changed occasionally—for instance, by slight variations at the monthly recollections; but I think it is important that we should never get away entirely from our retreat program unless we are faced with entirely new difficulties that demand our undivided attention.

Some may object that the plan is too negative. To this I can answer only that confession is supposed to deal with the negative side of our lives and that I have not proposed this plan as a complete enunciation of our spiritual ideals. And I might add that, if used perseveringly, the plan is very *positive* in its results. It makes for an increase of grace through the sacrament, for greater purity of conscience, and, incidentally, for helpful spiritual direction by the confessor.

chapter 7

Contrition

THE Council of Trent authoritatively declared that
true contrition consists in a detestation of one's sins,
with grief of soul, and a purpose of sinning no more.
According to the same Council, contrition is so necessary that God never forgives any personal sin, even in
the sacraments of baptism and penance, unless the
sinner genuinely repents.

Perhaps it is this doctrine of the necessity of contrition that makes the subject interesting. At any
rate, it *is* interesting. Anyone who has taught the subject, whether in a theology class or in an advanced
religion class, knows that. And we all know it from
personal experience, too. We want to be rid of our
sins; therefore we want to be sorry for them, and we
want to be sure we are sorry for them.

KINDS OF CONTRITION

Perfect Contrition

Perfect contrition is a subject of special interest
because it sometimes happens that perfect contrition
affords the only possible means of saving one's soul.
The baptized person who is in the state of mortal sin

and is dying without the opportunity of going to confession or receiving extreme unction is faced with the
grim alternative of making an act of perfect contrition or going to hell. The unbaptized sinner who is
dying without the opportunity of receiving actual
baptism faces a similar alternative.

No one can say that perfect contrition will never
be a matter of strict necessity for him, because mortal
sin is a possibility for everyone, and death without a
priest is also. Yet, even if it were never of strict necessity, the act of perfect contrition is a beautiful prayer
and should be said often. It is certainly the best kind
of contrition for venial sins; and, with regard to mortal sins, it has the special power of restoring sanctifying grace to the soul immediately, thus making it
unnecessary to wait for the opportunity of going to
confession is order to regain God's friendship, to be
able to merit eternal life, and to be prepared for sud-
den death.

Instructed Catholics usually know the *fact* that perfect contrition immediately blots out mortal sin, but
not infrequently they misunderstand the *reason* for
this special power of perfect contrition. In fact, only
recently, in a book which was otherwise sound and
excellent, the statement was made that in the case
of a baptized person who has committed a mortal
sin, perfect contrition restores grace because it contains a desire for the sacrament of penance. This is
not the correct explanation. It is true, of course, that,
in the case referred to, perfect contrition must contain at least an implicit intention of going to confession; otherwise it would be a means of salvation

wholly independent of the sacrament and would excuse us entirely from God's precept of confessing the mortal sins committed after baptism. But this intention to receive the sacrament is not what gives perfect contrition its special efficacy. Even imperfect contrition must contain such an intention.

The real reason why perfect contrition instantly restores grace to the soul, even before we go to confession, is to be found in its *motive*. Perfect contrition is motivated by charity. The sinner turns to God with perfect love, and God repays love with love. As our Lord told us, God takes up His abode with those who love Him.

We are often asked whether it is difficult for one who has sinned mortally to make an act of perfect contrition. In answering the question we must have regard for several points. In the first place, neither perfect nor imperfect contrition calls for a definite degree of intensity or requires any certain amount of time. On the other hand, both kinds of contrition must contain an *appreciation* or *preference* of God which entirely excludes the will to commit mortal sin. In other words, the contrite sinner must prefer God to any personal satisfaction that would conflict with God's friendship. This disposition is required in all contrition for mortal sin; and it is *enough,* even for perfect contrition. I emphasize the fact that it is enough, because I believe that the impression is sometimes given that perfect contrition must exclude all attachment to sin. This impression is not accurate. Perfect contrition admits of degrees. The lowest degree contains preference for God over anything that conflicts with His friendship; and this does not necessarily exclude attachment to venial sin. In assisting dying sinners, it seems advisable to begin with the lowest degree. After giving them the motive for perfect contrition—of which we shall speak in a moment—get them to repent of their mortal sins and to resolve never again to sin mortally. If they have this disposition, they have what is strictly necessary for "loving God above all things," for loving God "with their whole heart, their whole soul, and their whole mind." Having helped them to this essential disposition, one can then try to "go higher"—that is, to instill sorrow for venial sin and even to incite a desire for perfect conformity to the will of God in all things.

Under many aspects, therefore, an act of perfect contrition is not more difficult than imperfect contrition. The difficulty, insofar as there is a difficulty, lies in the one element that distinguishes perfect contrition from imperfect: namely, in the *motive*. Perfect contrition springs from charity; and charity is the love of God "for His own sake"—an unselfish, disinterested love. To love God for His own sake should not be difficult for anyone who really knows God—that is, for one who has come to appreciate through prayer that God is good and lovable; but for those who have given little thought to God, the case is probably different. They need to make some consideration that will show them that God is really worth loving for His own sake.

A rather simple way of helping a sinner to arrive at the motive necessary for perfect contrition is to get him to reflect on Christ Crucified. In our Lord on the Cross we have a very graphic portrayal of

God's love for us. Appreciation of this fact begets gratitude in the soul; and it is an easy step from gratitude to perfect love, the love of charity. St. John, the great apostle of charity, told us to follow this path from gratitude to charity when he said: "Let us therefore love God, because God first hath loved us" (I John 4:19). St. Paul's great personal love of our Lord sprang from an appreciation of the tremendous fact expressed in his words: "He loved me and delivered himself up for me." St. Francis Xavier's prayer of love *O Deus, Ego Amo Te* is a poetic expression of the words of St. John and of St. Paul. St. Ignatius, in his "Contemplation for Obtaining Love," uses the same psychology: he takes us from gratitude to perfect, unselfish, disinterested love. First we count the gifts of God to us, and, seeing their number and their value, we are deeply grateful; then, through the gifts, which are so good, we rise to the consideration of the infinite goodness of the Giver.

When we say that perfect contrition is motivated by charity and that charity is the love of God for His own sake, we do not mean that perfect contrition *excludes* all other motives. It is quite proper for us to be grateful to God for his benefits, to desire to enjoy the happiness of heaven, and to fear the punishments of hell. All such truths furnish motivation for sorrow for sin, and they can exist in the soul together with the motive for perfect contrition.

Imperfect Contrition

Perfect contrition is indeed excellent; but we should not overlook the value of imperfect contrition. Imperfect contrition is not enough of itself to

[151]

do away with mortal sin, yet even for those in the state of mortal sin it is very profitable. It disposes them to go to confession or to make an act of perfect contrition, and in confession it is a sufficient disposition for absolution.

As for venial sins, theologians commonly teach that imperfect contrition is enough for their remission outside of confession. Hence, those who have only venial sins on their souls need not be particularly solicitous about their motives when they make an act of contrition; any one of the many possible supernatural motives for detesting their sins will be a sufficient basis for a fruitful act of contrition.

ELEMENTS OF ALL CONTRITION

Since it is of little avail to consider the necessity and kinds of contrition if one's notion of contrition itself is not clear, it will be worth our while to return to the first sentence of this chapter. I indicated there that, according to the Council of Trent, all contrition contains three elements: detestation, grief, and purpose of amendment. And, of course, as a prerequisite to any act of contrition, there must be the realization that one has done wrong. Hence, every act of contrition includes in some way four psychological steps: we *realize* that we have sinned; we *detest* what we have done; we *grieve* over it; and we *resolve* to amend.

Though I should not want to encourage anyone to be technical in his prayers, I think we can all profit by occasionally taking apart an act of contrition, thinking over the meaning of each of these psychological steps and actually making the steps slowly and prayerfully. In the subsequent paragraphs, my purpose is to offer some explanations and suggestions that might help one who wants to make an act of contrition meditatively.

Perhaps I ought to preface my remarks with a brief statement concerning their doctrinal value. The Church has made it quite clear that an act of contrition must contain certain elements, but she has left the detailed explanation of these elements to her theologians. I have drawn my explanations from the works of eminent theologians; yet I realize that on some points the theological literature is somewhat obscure and that differences of opinion are permissible. In all cases of obscurity or uncertainty, I have aimed to limit my suggestions to what is safe and practicable.

Realization

When we make an act of contrition we have to be conscious of the fact *that we ourselves have done evil.* This supposes, undoubtedly, a speculative appreciation of the evil of sin, but it does not stop with mere speculation. The purpose of the realization which precedes and motivates the act of contrition is to get the sinner to turn away from his own sins, with grief and a purpose of amendment. Therefore, it is well to begin a meditative act of contrition with a consciousness of one's own sins. This does not necessarily mean a detailed examination of conscience, but it does imply at least a general recalling of one's sins.

In our catechism we say that an act of contrition

must be *supernatural*; that is, it must be made with God's grace and it must be based on a motive drawn from revelation. We may take it for granted that God gives the grace, but we ourselves have to supply the supernatural motive by considering our sins in the light of some revealed truth. Among the many truths that help to show us the evil of our sins, I might suggest the following:

The joys of heaven, or the pains of hell. These are directly applicable to mortal sin, because mortal sin deprives us of our right to heaven and makes us deserving of hell. But the thought of heaven can also be applied to venial sin because, after all, there are degrees of glory in heaven, and venial sin keeps us from attaining a higher degree of glory. The thought of hell can be used as a motive for repenting of even venial sin, because by committing venial sins we might form habits that would lead to mortal sin or lose certain special graces that would at times be necessary to overcome serious temptations. Of course, a consideration of purgatory, especially as a painful delay in reaching our heavenly home, is directly applicable to venial sin.

The glories of sanctifying grace. Grace makes our souls beautiful in the eyes of God; it makes us His adopted children, sharers in His nature, heirs to His happiness. Mortal sin loses this priceless possession for us; venial sin, though it does not affect the grace in our souls, represents a lost opportunity to grow in grace.

The Passion of our Lord. This furnishes fine motivation for sorrow for either mortal or venial sin. The same may be said for any aspect of our Lord's life, because everything we know about Him is calculated to increase our admiration and love of Him and thus show us by contrast the meanness of our failure to live according to the pattern He has given us.

The doctrine of the Redemption and of our part in it. God has so united us among ourselves that we can help one another in the way of salvation and sanctification. An appreciation of this truth and of its tremendous implications gives us a new light on sin: it is not only harmful to ourselves, it is a refusal to cooperate in a glorious cause.

The divine wisdom and goodness. Properly understood, this is the most all-embracing and fundamental and, I might add, the simplest of motives for detesting sin. It takes us back to the one reason why we and this whole world exist at all: namely, to share in the divine goodness according to the infinitely wise plan of God Himself. By sin, we do what we can to thwart His plan; we voluntarily prevent Him from giving Himself to us as He wishes.

Detestation

The whole purpose of meditating on one of the foregoing truths, or on some similar revealed truth, is to prepare the soul for an act of contrition. In the act of contrition itself, the first step is *detestation*.

Theologians generally agree, I believe, that, as a distinct element in the act of contrition, detestation refers to the past. The sinner goes back, so to speak, on the act that he performed and deliberately chooses to do just the opposite from what he did when he sinned. In sinning, he chose his own will in preference to God's will; now he turns away from his former choice and unites his will to God's.

Evidently we cannot undo an act that has been done. We can make reparation for it; we can pay damages; we can sometimes stop its effects; but the fact that it was committed cannot be changed. The most we can do with regard to a past act is wish we had not done it. And that seems the best way to describe detestation of sin: "I sincerely wish I had never done it."

In making a meditative act of contrition, it is probably not advisable to spend a great deal of time on this point. There is no direct way of testing an interior disposition such as detestation; and we are likely to be disturbed, and even frightened, by our sense-love and our self-love. Since these causes of sin are just as strong as they were when the sin was committed and since they keep telling us they liked the sin and are glad it happened, dwelling long on this point would make us think we have no contrition at all. It is better to make a simple act of the will ("Because I now see the evil that I did, I wish I had not committed it") and then go on to the next point. In practice, we can take the required detestation for granted if we have the realization, grief, and purpose of amendment.

Grief of Soul

The blessed in heaven can detest their sins but cannot grieve over them. The reason for this is that grief supposes the *presence* of an evil, and the sins of the blessed are merely *past* acts, the evil effects of which have all been removed.

With us, the case is different. For instance, when a man commits a mortal sin, his soul immediately becomes an object of reproach before God. This is an evil effect of sin over which he can certainly grieve. After he has made a good confession, he can have a reasonable assurance that he has regained God's friendship, but he is not sure that all the effects of his sin are removed. There may be some temporal punishment to undergo; there may be some weakness in the soul, some special liability to sin, that results from his former sin. Because of the possibility that such evil effects may continue, we can grieve over our sins all through our lives, for this possibility keeps the sins *present* to us at least in some sense.

Perhaps the best way to describe the grief of soul which constitutes the second element of contrition is to say that it is a desire to get rid of, to shake off, the effects of our sins, because we realize that in these effects our detestable sins still cling to us.

We have to remind good people again and again that grief over sin is not necessarily a matter of feeling. To use an illustration, let us suppose that two men get their hands and arms covered with mud. The first man likes mud and enjoys being covered with it; the second man does not like it. Then suppose that while they are covered with this particular mud they find out that it is very harmful to the skin. Both of them immediately try to wash it off. The example illustrates the difference between accidental grief and essential grief. Only one of the men had a *feeling* of repugnance for the mud, yet both of them tried to be rid of it when they found it was harmful. So it is with sorrow for sin. To *feel* grief over the effects of sin is good, and may even be called an accidental perfection of contrition; but the essential thing is to want to be rid of the evil.

The best expression of grief, therefore, is not tears, but the sincere will to go to confession, make an act of perfect contrition, gain indulgences, repair the injury done to one's neighbor, accept some hardship willingly in reparation for one's sins, or do some voluntary penance for the same purpose. These are the means of doing away with the effects of our sins; hence the will to do such things is a tangible way of showing ourselves that we are sorry, no matter how we feel.

Purpose of Amendment

Purpose of amendment, though by no means the whole of contrition, is a very important part of it and probably the best practical proof of it. No one can have real contrition unless he intends to amend his life; but, as this amendment can have different meanings for different cases, it may be well for us to consider some examples of these variations.

Suppose that a man who has committed mortal sins since his last confession now wants to regain the state of grace. Whether he goes to confession or makes an act of perfect contrition with the intention of going to confession, he must certainly be resolved to amend his life. And since his contrition concerns mortal sins, his purpose of amendment must be really *abso-*

lute: that is, he must intend to avoid *all* mortal sin in the future. He would have to have the same uncompromising resolution even if he had committed only one mortal sin. The "purpose of sinning no more" applies quite literally to the case of mortal sin.

On the other hand, imagine the case of a man who has committed only venial sins since his last confession, but who now wishes to make an act of contrition for *all* his venial sins because he wants to gain a plenary indulgence. What kind of purpose of amendment must this man have? It is hard to give a perfectly satisfactory answer to the question, but a safe one would seem to be that it is sufficient for him if he retains no attachment to any venial sins (in the sense that he intends to continue to commit *those* sins) and has at least a general intention to improve —for example, by reducing the number of his venial sins. We might add that it is generally recommended that such a man should center his purpose of amendment on the correction of something definite. This recommendation is given because experience teaches us that a general purpose of amendment is likely to prove ineffective and that the act of contrition in such a case is apt to degenerate into a mere formula, a bit of wishful thinking, and nothing more.

A third case: A man has committed only venial sins since his last confession, and, though he knows he is not really contrite for some of them, he does wish to make a sincere act of contrition for the sins of lying. What must be this man's purpose of amendment? Again, the case is not easy to solve with perfect satisfaction, but it seems safe to give this practical

[159]

rule: If the man's lies are of the fully deliberate kind, he ought to be resolved to avoid them entirely; but if the lies are rather of the semi-deliberate kind, he ought at least to have the good will to try to reduce their number.

In the foregoing cases, "amendment of life" was used in its ordinary, everyday sense: that is, as an improvement over one's *recent* conduct. There is a fourth case, in which the expression evidently has a different meaning. Consider, for example, the holy King David. He offended God seriously; then he repented of that sin, was forgiven, and, as far as we know, lived many years in the friendship of God. Nevertheless, he continued to recite his *Miserere* for his past lapse from grace. It would be absurd to think that this *Miserere* was not a good act of contrition; but if it was an act of contrition, in what did the amendment consist? It seems obvious that "amendment" in such circumstances has a wide meaning: that is, it refers to the renewed purpose of *continuing* the reform that began years ago.

The case of David is repeated week after week in our confessionals throughout the world. People sin mortally in their youth; they confess these sins, and then live for many years without further serious lapses. Still, they can certainly make acts of contrition for the old mortal sins; in fact, they are even advised to include these sins in their confessions so as to benefit more and more by the absolution. In their case, as in David's, the purpose of amendment for their mortal sins does not mean an intention to correct their present lives, but rather the renewed purpose to persevere in the amendment that has long since been brought about.

The examples illustrate the various aspects of and requisites for purpose of amendment. In our own case, when we make an act of contrition, we shall generally find a combination of these examples. We have sins of the past, for which it is sufficient to renew our purpose of amendment; and recent sins, which call for actual amendment and definite resolutions.

We saw that the feelings sometimes present a psychological difficulty in estimating detestation and grief. Something similar can happen with regard to purpose of amendment, particularly when habitual sins of frailty are involved. The sinner realizes his weakness and, even when he makes his act of contrition or goes to confession, feels sure he is going to sin again. Because of this, he wonders if he really has a purpose of amendment. The solution to the difficulty lies in a proper understanding of a purpose of amendment. It is not an act of the mind, but of the will. It is a sincere intention to try to amend, and to take the means necessary for doing that. The feeling that one will sin again may result, not from any ill will, but from the consciousness that one is weak and that this weakness has expressed itself again and again. But there is no weakness that cannot be overcome by serious effort and the grace of God. Even the most habitual sinner can resolve to make the effort, and he may be sure that God will give the grace. He should not be discouraged if he does fall again for such a fall may simply be a sign that he has not yet discovered the proper means for correcting his particular bad habit.

Sometimes people think they will automatically overcome bad habits if only they go to the sacraments frequently. This is but one aspect of the solution, and it will never work unless the sinner takes the more obvious means of avoiding occasions of sin, of exercising himself in self-control, and so forth.

My analysis of the act of contrition has been long. Yet I hope it contains some helpful suggestions. In particular, I think that many would find it fruitful to make a meditative act of contrition occasionally—for example, during the morning meditation on confession day. The Church evidently wants us to draw great profit from frequent confession, and for this there is no means more effective than an increase in contrition.

chapter 8

The Prudent Use of
Confession Privileges

THERE was a time when religious were severely limited as to their choice of confessors. More recent legislation has very wisely mitigated those restrictions; and the Code of Canon Law guarantees to religious many privileges of confessing, under certain circumstances, to priests other than those appointed as their ordinary confessors. Since the promulgation of the Code much has been written to explain the meaning and extent of these privileges, but comparatively little has been said about their prudent use. I believe it should be very profitable to consider the legislation under this latter aspect. For the sake of clarity, I shall first consider the confessors of sisters and then apply my remarks, with the needed qualifications, to the confessors of religious men.

CONFESSORS OF SISTERS

The Ordinary Confessor

The concept of the ordinary confessor of sisters, according to the mind of the Church, is basic to this

[163]

entire subject. He is not to be a *mere* confessor. This expression might sound shocking if taken out of its context. Penance is a sacrament, and as a sacrament it is productive of graces which in themselves are more fruitful for the human soul than is spiritual counsel. The greatest work that a priest does in the confessional is to give absolution. There should be no mistake about that point; the sacramental value of absolution should never be placed below spiritual advice, and the first purpose of every penitent should be to perfect his disposition for the fruitful reception of the sacrament.

Religious, however, are not ordinary penitents. They belong to the spiritual elite of the Church. They are supposed to strive after perfection, and they are entitled to the means conducive to perfection. One of these means is the opportunity of having expert spiritual guidance. True, to some extent this guidance is embodied in their rule, for the rule contains the plan of a perfect life. Also, guidance is frequently available through their superiors. Despite these helps, however, all will experience, at least at times, the need of counsel which only a priest can give.

It is the mind of the Church that in each community of sisters this priestly counsel should be given normally by the ordinary confessor. In making this legislation, the Church intends to provide the sisters with direction that is capable, consistent, and uniform. It should be capable because of their special position in the Church; it should be consistent because this quality is generally needed for progress;

and it should be at least relatively uniform because of their uniform manner of life, in which, owing to very close contact, great differences of direction could make for disagreeable situations.

Such is the ideal. It is not always realized in practice. Ecclesiastical superiors have no special charism that prevents them from making mistakes in their appointments; and at times they must appoint ordinary confessors who, they realize, do not measure up perfectly to the canonical standards. Like the rest of us, they cannot give what they do not have. In these situations the sisters must be both fair-minded and patient. If possible, they can avail themselves of the other privileges given by canon law; when this is impossible, they have every reason to trust in God.

Extraordinary and Retreat Confessors

The Church also prescribes that sisters have an extraordinary confessor, and a practically universal custom provides yet another confessor at the time of retreat. It may be well to consider just what use the sisters are expected to make of these opportunities.

Regarding the extraordinary confessor, it is not expected that everyone will wish his advice, nor should it be expected that he will volunteer direction to all. He is given to all in order to safeguard the opportunity of the few who may need his help. In a community in which all find the ordinary confessor satisfactory, the work of the extraordinary could well be limited to hearing the confessions and giving absolution.

The prudent use of the opportunity of consulting

the retreat confessor is a subject as difficult as it is delicate. Let me begin by stating that some sisters need this opportunity very much. They may have been in a small community all year, without an ordinary or extraordinary confessor in whom they had confidence and with relatively little opportunity of profiting by the various privileges accorded by canon law. Perhaps many problems have accumulated; perhaps, too, if they do not obtain help during the retreat in planning for the future, they will never get it. Sisters belonging to this class should feel perfectly free to discuss their problems and plans with the retreat confessor; and he, on his part, should be quite willing to give all the time and help he can.

The case is different with the sisters who have a good ordinary confessor during the year. All other things being equal, his guidance should be sought in preference to that of the retreat confessor. The sisters may say, of course, that at time of retreat they make a "yearly review." But does this review necessarily bring up new problems? Or, again, they may say that during retreat they must plan for the future and that in this planning they will need some guidance. This is true, but it can be overdone. They might discuss the general notion of this plan with their ordinary confessor before they leave for retreat. Unless the retreat is marked by very special inspirations, one can usually predict ahead of time along what line one is going to need a renovation of spirit. Furthermore, when the plan is made, is it not better to get the desired approbation from the priest who knows one and is to guide one in the keeping of it rather than from a priest one may never see again?

Special Confessor or Director

The foregoing are the confessional opportunities regularly provided for all. Many will find them sufficient for their needs and ideals; yet there will always be a few who will need the habitual help of another priest, and many who will rightly desire the opportunity of occasionally going to another. The Church has provided for both kinds of exceptions to the general rule; and we can consider now the right use of these exceptional privileges.

Roughly speaking, those sisters who wish the habitual help of another confessor may be divided into two classes that can be exemplified as follows. Sister A does not wish to go to the ordinary confessor at all; she wants a *substitute* confessor for herself. Sister B is willing to confess to the ordinary confessor at the customary times, but she also wishes to go to confession periodically (say, every week or every month) to another priest. To the ordinary priest, Sister B merely makes her confession; with the second, she discusses her spiritual life more in detail. In other words, Sister B wants an *extra* confessor, who is to serve mainly as her *spiritual adviser*.

Cases like these, though exceptions to the general rule, are not to be branded as singularities. Considering the wide differences of human temperament and human needs, it is not surprising that even an excellent ordinary confessor will not satisfy everybody.

The Code (in canon 520, § 2) takes cognizance of these diversities, by instructing the local ordinary to be gracious in granting the request of such sisters when they ask for a special confessor or director.

In making this wise provision, the Church is not catering to the mere whim or caprice of the sisters. They are to have a serious supernatural reason for making their request. In general, these reasons may be summed up as follows: the sister finds it extraordinarily difficult to manifest her conscience sincerely to the ordinary confessor, or she honestly judges that it would be to the greater good of her soul to have another confessor or director.

The canon law does not authorize the sister to appoint her own special confessor or director. The appointment should come from the local ordinary, upon her request. The request itself might take one of these two forms: the sister might merely ask for the special confessor or director and leave the choice to the local ordinary, or she might have a definite priest in mind and ask for him. In the second case she is not free from personal responsibility in making the choice. Naturally, the ordinary would not approve the choice if he knew the man to be incapable of fulfilling the office, but, on the other hand, he is not always able to discern the hidden motives that might lie behind such a request. The sister herself must judge that the choice is really for her spiritual good.

Extra-confessional Director

What of the sister who makes her confession to the ordinary confessor, but who wishes periodically to discuss the affairs of her soul with another priest, outside the confessional? Note that this case is different from that of Sister B, previously outlined. Sister B wanted direction in confession; in the case we are now considering the direction is entirely separated from the confessional.

A few eminent canonists think that, since the director in this case is not to serve as confessor to the sister, the case need not, strictly speaking, be referred to the local ordinary. It seems to me that, since this second priest is really to serve as the sister's spiritual director, he should be appointed by the ordinary. However, even those who, in a speculative way, hold the more lenient view on this one point admit that the case involves serious difficulties and demands special safeguards.

It is a generally recognized ascetical rule that the confessional is the proper place for the spiritual guidance of women. This rule is not absolute; it admits of exceptions, and no doubt there are cases in which a sister can receive more apt guidance outside the confessional. But the dangers involved should be recognized. If the Church demands certain qualities of virtue, prudence, and maturity of the ordinary confessor, with much greater reason would she demand them of an extra-confessional director. If there is danger of wasting time in the confessional, there is much greater danger of doing so outside. If an inordinate personal attachment might arise even from the confessional, there is much more danger of this when the safeguards of the confessional are abolished.

I would not want to be misunderstood in this mat-

[169]

ter. It is wrong to be constantly suspecting people, and much harm has come to many earnest souls through rash suspicions and rumors; but it is foolish, and may be quite wrong, for sisters to cherish the notion that, simply because they wish to discuss their spiritual life, these meetings never involve danger. In this matter, a bit of self-suspicion at the beginning can save a great deal of self-reproach at the end.

Whatever may be said theoretically about the need of the local ordinary's permission for this extra-confessional director, it is certain that no sister could adopt the practice of meeting her self-chosen, extra-confessional director without at least the permission of her own superior. The superior should weigh this question very carefully. In practice, she could seldom give a confident judgment without consulting the local ordinary, especially when the parties are young and the visits frequent.

Occasional Confessors

The number of sisters who desire a special confessor or director is comparatively small; the number of those who might want the opportunity of occasionally consulting another priest besides the ordinary confessor is rather large. To guarantee the latter as much liberty of conscience as possible, the canon law provides for *supplementary* and *occasional* confessors.

The supplementary confessors are appointed by the local ordinary, assigned to definite houses or groups of houses, and given the special jurisdiction required for hearing the confessions of religious women. The religious are free to summon any one of these or the extraordinary confessor. Not much need be said concerning the prudent use of this privilege. Since the confessors are designated by the bishop himself, it may be presumed that they will be capable men. The principal danger of abuse would come from the sister herself, were she to call for them without sufficient reason, at a needlessly inopportune time, or perhaps from an unreasonably long distance.

In a large city, the privilege of the supplementary confessors may have much practical value, but in general most sisters will find the very wide concession of canon 522 more useful. Canon 522 allows sisters to take advantage of the opportunity of confessing to any priest approved in the diocese for the confessions of women. The priest need not have the special approbation necessary for the confessors of sisters. The canon does not give permission to leave the house or to set aside the order of the house or the prescriptions of rule; but it does allow the sisters to take advantage of any legitimate opportunity of confessing when they are outside the house, as well as to a priest who happens to be visiting the convent, and it even allows them to call a priest to the convent. In all cases, the confession must be made in a place which conforms with the legislation of the Church for hearing the confessions of women.

One phrase in canon 522 calls for particular attention here. This privilege is accorded to the sister for her "peace of conscience." This phrase has been discussed and rediscussed by canonists. Authorities now commonly agree that any confession seriously made satisfies this demand insofar as the law is concerned.

But the spirit behind the law must be kept in mind when we are considering the prudent use of this privilege. Evidently, in framing this law, the Church did not wish to do away with all the prescriptions and counsels that she had laid down for the proper direction of sisters. Certainly she does not wish by this one canon to set aside the maxims of sound Catholic asceticism; and most certainly she does not wish to justify a departure from the more basic and necessary principles of moral theology.

From both the canonical and the ascetical points of view it is a mistake for a sister to go to another confessor for advice or to confess things that naturally call for advice, if her ordinary confessor would prove equally satisfactory. The difficulty proposed or the matter confessed may be the very thing that the ordinary confessor should know in order to give her progressive and helpful direction. Of course, there are occasions when the ordinary confessor is not available. If, after consulting another confessor under such circumstances, she goes over the matter later with her ordinary confessor, she will be acting according to a sound ascetical practice.

The mistake made in the use of this privilege can violate not merely ascetical principles, but also certain basic principles of moral theology. Perhaps we can illustrate by an example. Any priest knows that young people who are becoming addicted to certain bad habits are prone to "shop around," as the saying goes, for an "easy" confessor. In doing this they make two serious mistakes. They go from one confessor to another with the result that none of these transitory confessors can give them real help; and, when at last they settle on the easy one, they choose him precisely because he does not have the qualities that a helpful confessor should have.

Father B. van Acken, S.J., once pointed out that some religious who experience difficulties with regard to the religious life in general or with regard to one of the vows in particular, are apt to make this same childish mistake.[1] They need sympathetic direction, it is true, but also expert and firm direction. Because they fear this, they avail themselves of the privilege of canon 522 to shop around for a confessor who will ask no questions or make no firm demands of them. This is the gravest of all the abuses that can result from the imprudent use of the privilege. Needless to say, the Church never intended this favor to be a source of the loss of vocation and even a grave danger to the soul. Religious in extreme difficulties of this kind, more than any others, need the help of a man who knows the demands of the religious life. If they cannot get it, then God's grace must be sufficient for them; but if they deliberately avoid it, they expose their souls to extreme peril.

APPLICATION TO RELIGIOUS MEN

Provisions for confessors of religious men follow the same general lines as the legislation for sisters. In lay institutes of men there must be one ordinary and one extraordinary confessor for each house, and the local ordinary is to grant a special confessor to the

1 "Abusus libertatis religiosis pro confessione concessae," *Commentarium pro religiosis,* VII (1926), 255-260.

individual religious who asks for one. The Code says nothing about extraordinary and special confessors for professed members of clerical institutes, but it seems to be the common practice to provide these. All religious men may confess to their priest superiors who have confessional jurisdiction; and all have the privilege of confessing to any priest having the faculties of the diocese, even though not specially approved for religious.

The prudent use of these privileges is governed by the same general principles I have just explained in treating of the privileges of sisters. By way of brief and practical summary, we may say that these principles are aptly expressed by two words: *competence* and *consistency*.

As regards the principle of *competence,* religious must bear in mind that the Church, in allowing them to confess to all priests with diocesan faculties, does not thereby approve all these priests for the direction of religious. This applies not only to diocesan priests but also to members of one's own institute. Some lack the experience, the right attitude, or some other quality needed for sure guidance in certain delicate problems.

To be more concrete in a matter of such great importance, let me say quite candidly that there are some problems which a young religious must take particular pains to face and solve honestly. Notable among these may be mentioned a strongly rebellious spirit, a fundamental inability to live and work harmoniously with one's brethren, a genuine weakness in regard to sobriety or chastity. To embrace the religious state permanently and, above all, to go to ordination in the face of serious doubts in such matters is wrong. The competent confessor knows this and will put the proper alternatives squarely before his penitent. Another confessor might fail to recognize the case as truly serious or, if he does recognize it, might be too hesitant in prescribing the remedy. The grave results of what is falsely termed "kindness" in this matter are too well known to need comment.

As for the principle of *consistency,* I have already indicated that, even in the ordinary affairs of the spiritual life, it is unwise to shift confessors or directors needlessly. In serious matters such as those mentioned above, this shifting will amount to gross imprudence if it means that a religious goes from one confessor to another to such an extent that even a competent confessor would not have the opportunity of recognizing a difficulty as habitual.

Conclusion

Although some of the statements made in this chapter may sound rather severe, I did not make them with the intention of minimizing the privileges granted by the Church. Rather, my one desire was to make these privileges more useful by showing how they fit into the entire scheme of canonical legislation and approved asceticism.

chapter 9

Confession Before Communion

On the fifteenth of June, 1520, in a memorable document which begins with the words *Exsurge Domine (Arise, O Lord)*, Pope Leo X condemned a multitude of errors of Martin Luther. Among these errors was Luther's teaching on the preparation required for Holy Communion. According to him, prayers and other pious works, as well as contrition for mortal sin and even confession itself, are useless; all that is required is to believe, to have confidence that one will obtain grace in the sacrament, and this alone will make one pure and worthy.

Thirty-one years later, in its thirteenth session (October 11, 1551), the Council of Trent considered this same erroneous teaching, and stated the true doctrine in a chapter and a canon. Entitled "On the preparation to be given that one may worthily receive the sacred Eucharist," chapter VII runs as follows:

> If it is unbeseeming for anyone to approach to any of the sacred functions unless he approach holily; assuredly, the more the holiness and divinity of this heavenly sacrament are understood by a Christian, the more diligently ought he to give heed that he approach not to receive it but with great reverence and holiness,

especially as we read in the Apostle those words full of terror: *He that eateth and drinketh unworthily, eateth and drinketh judgment to himself.* Wherefore, he who would communicate ought to recall to mind the precept of the Apostle: *Let a man prove himself.* Now ecclesiastical usage declares that necessary proof to be, that no one, conscious to himself of mortal sin, how contrite soever he may seem to himself, ought to approach to the sacred Eucharist without previous sacramental confession. This the holy Synod hath decreed is to be invariably observed by all Christians, even by those priests on whom it may be incumbent by their office to celebrate, provided the opportunity of a confessor do not fail them; but if, in an urgent necessity, a priest should celebrate without previous confession, let him confess as soon as possible." [1]

The eleventh canon of the same session makes explicit reference to the Lutheran error. It reads:

If anyone saith, that faith alone is a sufficient preparation for receiving the sacrament of the most holy Eucharist; let him be anathema. And for fear lest so great a sacrament may be received unworthily, and so unto death and condemnation, this holy Synod ordains and declares that sacramental confession, when a confessor may be had, is of necessity to be made beforehand, by those whose conscience is burthened with mortal sin, how contrite even soever they may think themselves. But if anyone shall presume to teach, preach, or obstinately to assert, or even in public dis-

[1] J. Waterworth, *The Canons and Decrees of the Sacred and Oecumenical Council of Trent* (New York: Dunigan, 1848), pp. 80-81.

putation to defend the contrary, he shall be thereupon excommunicated.[2]

The foregoing teaching of the Council of Trent is the principal source of our present canon law; namely, canon 807, which concerns the celebration of Mass; and canon 856, which concerns the reception of Holy Communion. An English version of the latter canon runs as follows: "No one with a mortal sin on his conscience is to receive holy Communion without previous sacramental confession, no matter how contrite he may deem himself to be. In a case of urgent necessity, however, and when no confessor is available, he must first make an act of perfect contrition."

This law is of the greatest moment. It should be clearly understood by religion teachers, catechists, and frequent communicants. Properly to understand it, one must have a grasp of these three propositions: (I) It is *always* necessary to be in the state of grace when receiving Holy Communion. (II) It is *almost always* necessary to confess before receiving Holy Communion if one has committed a mortal sin since one's last good confession. (III) In certain *extraordinary* circumstances it is sufficient to regain grace by an act of perfect contrition before receiving Holy Communion. The purpose of the present chapter is to explain these three propositions and (IV) to call attention to some precautions to be taken in order to safeguard the ordinary observance of the law and avoid sacrilegious Communions.

[2] *Ibid.*, p. 84.

I. IT IS ALWAYS NECESSARY TO BE IN THE STATE OF GRACE WHEN RECEIVING COMMUNION

One reason for this is that the Holy Eucharist is a sacrament of the living. A sacrament of the living supposes its recipient to be already supernaturally alive—that is, living the divine life of grace—and its function is to increase this divine life in the soul. A second reason is found in the special purpose of the Eucharist, which is to *nourish*. We do not speak of nourishing a corpse; nourishment supposes that life already exists.

The conscious reception of Holy Communion while in the state of mortal sin is a grave sacrilege. It is to receive the source of salvation unto one's own condemnation. No one, therefore, should receive this sacrament unless he has a reasonable assurance that he is in the state of grace. I say "a reasonable assurance" because when there is question of our interior state of soul it is not possible for us, apart from a special divine revelation, to have an absolute certainty that we are in the state of grace. All that God expects of us in this and similar matters is a practical, or working, certainty that we fulfill various conditions established by Himself or the Church for His honor and our own spiritual welfare. For ordinary people there is no difficulty in this matter. They go to confession, do what they can to fulfill the requisites of a good confession, and leave the confessional in peace, sufficiently confident that their sins are forgiven and that they are in the state of grace. And the same is true of them when they make an act of perfect contrition: they are reasonably, or practically, sure that through this act they are restored to God's friendship, in case they had lost it through mortal sin.

(Contrition, said the Council of Trent, is perfect through charity. Hence, perfect contrition is sorrow for sin based upon a motive of charity; that is, sorrow because one has offended God, who is the supreme good and worthy to be loved above all things. It is not difficult for those who are accustomed to think of God to make an act of perfect contrition and to mean it. The formula for the act of contrition, as ordinarily taught in catechism classes, contains both imperfect and perfect contrition. This is appropriate, because sorrow for the perfect motive does not exclude sorrow for lesser motives.)

Some people, such as the scrupulous, have great difficulty in these matters. They always feel spiritually insecure. No matter what their reason might tell them of their state of soul, its calm judgment is stifled by their fear; and this fear makes them *feel* that they are not, or may not be, in the state of grace. If such people were to follow their feelings, they would very likely never receive a sacrament of the living, especially the Holy Eucharist. For them it is necessary to follow sound direction in spite of their feelings—all the while working towards the goal of being able to make quiet judgments for themselves, judgments based on facts and not on fear.

As is true of other sins, one must realize what he is doing in order to be guilty of a sacrilegious Communion. Consequently, one who is actually in the

[181]

state of mortal sin but does not advert to this when he receives Holy Communion does not commit a sin; in fact, it may be that he receives sanctifying grace through the Eucharist itself. Many eminent theologians hold that a sinner (that is, one in the state of mortal sin) who receives Holy Communion in good faith and with imperfect contrition for his sins is restored to grace through this sacrament. Knowledge of this opinion may be a consolation to those who are apt to worry about being deprived of grace because of unsuspected unworthiness when they communicate.

Instances of receiving Holy Communion without adverting to the fact that one is in the state of mortal sin can hardly be very common; but this is certainly not an impossibility, especially for some people whose devotions are governed by routine. For example, suppose that a layman is accustomed to receive Holy Communion the first Sunday of every month and to go to confession the day before. It might happen that something unforeseen would prevent his going to confession, and then, following his routine pattern, he would communicate Sunday morning without realizing at the time that he had been unable to make his usual confession. If he had committed a mortal sin and made only an act of imperfect contrition, he would still be in mortal sin at the time of communicating. Being unconscious of this, he would be in what is called "good faith." Communion would probably have the same effect for him as an act of perfect contrition—namely, give him sanctifying grace, though he would still be obliged to confess his sin.

II. IT IS ALMOST ALWAYS NECESSARY TO CONFESS BEFORE RECEIVING COMMUNION IF ONE HAS COMMITTED A MORTAL SIN SINCE ONE'S LAST GOOD CONFESSION

To say that one must be in the state of grace when receiving a sacrament of the living is not the same as saying that a sinner must go to confession before receiving one of these sacraments. It is possible to regain sanctifying grace either through actual confession or through perfect contrition, which includes the intention to confess at the proper time. Nothing in the nature of a sacrament of the living makes actual confession a necessary prerequisite; nor is there any special law which makes confession necessary, except for the Holy Eucharist. For instance, if a young man who is to be confirmed tomorrow commits a mortal sin today, he is certainly obliged to regain sanctifying grace before receiving confirmation, but an act of perfect contrition would suffice for this purpose. This would be true also of matrimony, holy orders, and extreme unction, if these sacraments were received apart from Holy Communion or the celebration of Mass.

The Holy Eucharist, therefore, is governed by an entirely special law. As we learn from the Council of Trent and the Code, the regaining of grace through perfect contrition is not normally sufficient for the reception of this sacrament; sacramental confession is ordinarily required. The reason for this seems to be the entirely special character of the Holy Eucharist. It is the most excellent of sacraments, and it is

[183]

to be safeguarded as much as is humanly possible against the danger of abuse.

Is this law prescribing confession before Communion a divine law or a law made by the Church? The answer to this question is not clear. Some of the greatest of post-Tridentine theologians explain it as a divine law promulgated through St. Paul. St. Alphonsus Liguori, writing in the eighteenth century, adheres to this explanation as being by far the more common and the only true one. Nevertheless, eminent modern theologians express dissatisfaction with the arguments that the law is of divine origin and hold that the words of the Council of Trent are sufficiently verified if the law is considered to be of ecclesiastical origin. In either case—whether divine or merely ecclesiastical—the law is strictly binding, and the only exception to it is officially declared by the Church to be a case in which Communion is necessary and confession is impossible, as will be explained in our next section.

Who are obliged by this law to go to confession before receiving Communion? *Only those who are certain that they have committed a mortal sin since their last good confession.* Therefore, one who inculpably failed to tell a mortal sin in an otherwise good confession is not obliged to abstain from Communion until he makes another confession. He has already regained grace through confession. It is true, of course, that the omitted sin must still be confessed; but it is not necessary to advance one's ordinary time of confession in order to do this, and in the meantime one may receive Holy Communion

[184]

even daily as long as he commits no further mortal sin.

It is clear that if one who *knows* he forgot to tell a mortal sin in confession may receive Holy Communion, then one who merely *doubts* whether he forgot to tell a sin has the same privilege. But what of one who knows he committed a mortal sin and doubts whether he has been to confession at all since then (not a very common case), or of one who doubts whether he has sinned mortally (for example, by sufficient reflection or full consent) since his last confession? Regarding these cases there would be some difference of opinion among theologians; but a sound practical rule covering all such doubts is this: the sole obligation is to take some available means of removing the doubt so that one will be reasonably sure of being in the state of grace when receiving Holy Communion.

Sometimes what is called a doubt is not a doubt at all, but merely a scruple or a sort of hazy fear. The best treatment for such worries is to pay as little heed as possible to them, even though they accompany the holiest of actions. In other instances, a doubt is a sort of temporary state of mind that can be corrected by the application of a sound rule of presumption. For instance, one who wonders whether he gave full consent in some very disturbing temptation, might realize in his calmer moments that in similar situations he never, or practically never, gives in to the temptation. Thus the presumption of not consenting favors him, and he may use this presumption to dispel his perplexity and to form the practical judgment that he is still in the state of grace. In such cases neither confession nor perfect contrition is strictly required before Holy Communion.

But it may happen occasionally to anyone that his doubt whether he has committed a mortal sin is too solidly founded to be ignored and that the circumstances of the temptation are so unusual that the ordinary presumptions are not helpful. In other words, one might have a really sincere and insoluble doubt whether he is here and now in the state of mortal sin. Even in this case confession is not obligatory; but if one does not wish to go to confession, one should make an act of perfect contrition before receiving Communion. According to some good authors, even the act of perfect contrition is not strictly necessary; but it is hard to find any sound reason for this opinion, and I would not sponsor it. On the other hand, many, if not most, authors think that confession is generally advisable in these cases of insoluble doubt. For myself, I would be very slow to recommend the special confession of doubtful sins except to persons who might need this as a means of correcting a proneness to laxity.

III. IN CERTAIN EXTRAORDINARY CIRCUM- STANCES IT IS SUFFICIENT TO REGAIN GRACE BEFORE RECEIVING COMMUNION BY MAKING AN ACT OF PERFECT CONTRITION

A problem proposed to Father Michael O'Donnell [3] can aptly introduce the present section. The problem concerns "a person who did an impure action and

[3] *Moral Questions* (Dublin: Golden Eagle Books, 1945), p. 270.

was heartily sorry for doing so, and wanted to receive Our Blessed Lord the following morning." This
person evidently had no opportunity to go to confession; hence he made an act of perfect contrition
"and promised Our Lord he would go to confession
at the first opportunity and tell that sin of impurity
and fulfilled that promise a few days later." He now
wants to know whether he did wrong in going to
Communion.

This is a very *human* problem. One can almost
feel the anxiety of the questioner. Father O'Donnell
rightly sets his mind at rest by saying that, since he
acted in good faith, he has no need to worry. It is
one thing, however, to decide whether one has been
guilty of sin, another thing to tell one what to do in
the future. It cannot be repeated too often that past
actions are not to be judged by present knowledge.
Many of us have done things in perfectly good faith
which we later learned were forbidden. In acting
thus we were not guilty of sin; in fact, we may have
been highly pleasing to God because we did what
we thought was right under the circumstances. So,
too, we may have done things in a sort of perplexed
state, having tried the best we could to decide what
was right, and then acted, but with a sort of vague
anxiety. This is not what authors refer to when they
condemn acting "in practical doubt." The "practical
doubter" is not merely troubled by a vague worry or
perplexity; he is one who has a serious reason for
questioning whether what he is about to do is sinful
and then, without forming his conscience, does it
anyway.

I call attention to this principle that past actions

are not to be judged by present knowledge, because it is not entirely unlikely that some of my readers may have had an experience similar to that of Father O'Donnell's questioner. Lacking a clear knowledge of the law of confession before Communion, they may have received Communion without previous confession in some instance in which, according to the explanation given here, they were not justified in doing so. Let them be content to use the new knowledge as a guide for the future and not make it a cause of anxiety about the past.

Many laws admit of exceptions by reason of some extraordinary circumstances or combination of circumstances. Thus, a mother who must care for a sick child is excused from Sunday Mass; the poor who live on what they receive from others are excused from the law of abstinence; and so forth. The law prescribing confession before Communion also admits of exception, but the Church considers this matter of such importance that she officially declares just what circumstances constitute the exception. For a legitimate exception there must be a combination of two extraordinary circumstances: (1) *impossibility of going to confession*; and (2) *necessity of receiving Communion*. Both conditions must be verified. And both need some explanation.

1. *Confession Impossible*

Authors generally illustrate this matter with the example of a person who is already kneeling at the Communion rail before he realizes that he should have gone to confession. It is clear that if he is to receive Communion now (whether that is necessary will be treated later), then confession before Communion is impossible. He cannot stop the priest at the altar rail and say: "Will you please hear my confession before giving me Communion?"

Father Edwin F. Healy, S.J.,[4] uses the example of a father of a family who has planned on receiving Communion with his children on their mother's anniversary. He intends to go to confession before Mass, but when they reach the church they find that the only priest of this parish is already beginning Mass. As Father Healy points out, it would be out of the question for the man to leave church and go elsewhere to confession if he is to receive Communion with his family at this Mass.

Examples of inability to get to confession are not limited to these last-minute cases. The impossibility might last for some time, especially in a small town when the pastor is absent and when inclement weather or lack of time would prevent one from going to another town. Moreover, there may be cases in which confession is impossible although a priest can be reached; for example, if the priest will not hear the confession, perhaps because of scrupulosity. Or the only available priest might not have the faculties to hear confessions. This would not be very common in our country; but it could happen, for instance, in the case of a priest outside his own diocese. It would be more common in some countries where it is customary to limit the jurisdiction of young priests to a certain class of persons.

4 *Christian Guidance* (Chicago: Loyola University, 1949), p. 105.

At the time of the Council of Trent the limitation of confessional faculties was not at all uncommon; hence cases in which an available priest might be unable to hear one's confession were not rare. This seems to be one reason for the rather strange wording used by the Council in declaring the law of confessing before Communion. Confession is necessary, it says, if one has a *"copia confessoris."* The Code preserves the same expression, *"copia confessarii."* The literal meaning of *copia* is "a plenty, an abundance," and the very use of the expression implies that it might be possible to have a priest present, yet no confessor available. Various authors try to express this idea by saying that confession is necessary: if a confessor is present to whom one is obliged to confess; if a suitable confessor is present; if there is an available priest to whom one could go to confession without grave inconvenience.

The foregoing are various ways of saying that even when a priest is present or can be reached confession may be a practical impossibility. I have already cited two examples of this: the priest who cannot hear the confession, and the priest who will not hear it. Another example of this practical impossibility of confessing is the case in which confession cannot be made with the necessary privacy. Still another case, very clear in theory but not nearly so clear in its application, is that in which the very going to confession would create suspicion in the minds of others that one had sinned seriously. I say this is clear in theory because such a danger to one's reputation is certainly an extraordinary inconvenience that would make confession morally impossible; and I add that it is not clear in its practical application because the danger is more likely to exist merely in the minds of certain oversensitive individuals than in actual fact. It is sometimes said that this kind of situation is not uncommon in communities of sisters, so that a sister who would go to confession before Mass would be open to suspicion. Perhaps there are some communities in which such gross unkindness and injustice prevail, but we can at least hope that they are very rare and that they will soon reform.

Theologians discuss and dispute over what they call the "invincible repugnance" attached to going to confession to a certain individual. All agree, of course, that the mere difficulty of confession, or the mere humiliation of confessing a serious sin—difficulties inherent in confession to some extent for most people—would not constitute a moral impossibility of going to confession. The debatable case concerns repugnance or embarrassment that arises from some kind of special relationship with the confessor. This might be blood relationship: for example, the confessor is one's son or brother. It might be a relationship of work: for example, the confessor and the penitent are working intimately together day after day. Or it might be a relationship—if I may use the term—of dislike. Let us suppose that a certain priest clearly dislikes me and loses no opportunity of showing it by being rude or by ridiculing me. It is easily seen that I might have a repugnance to confessing a serious sin to that priest which would be entirely *special*, entirely different from the difficulty normally experienced in confession.

No one holds that these relationships always create

"invincible repugnance." But many theologians believe that this psychological effect is experienced in some cases and that, in these cases, there is a truly extraordinary inconvenience which amounts to a moral impossibility of confessing to a particular priest. Hence, they would say that, if such a priest were the only one available, confession would be a practical impossibility. I am convinced that these theologians are correct; and I believe that St. Thomas Aquinas would agree with them, too. With reference to a similar question—the necessity of making the annual confession "to one's own priest"—St. Thomas recommended great liberality in allowing people to go to other confessors, "because," he said, "many are so weak that they would rather die without confession than confess to that priest." [5]

A few other cases generally cited by authors as constituting an impossibility of confessing are these: the danger of scandalizing the priest; the danger that confessional secrecy will be abused; the danger of revealing one's accomplice in a sin. Granted that such conditions existed, they would make confession morally impossible; but I think their actual existence would be rare.

2. *Communion Necessary*

Because of the variety of situations which make confession a moral impossibility, the first condition for the exception to the law of confession before Communion is not entirely uncommon. But a second condition is also required—the *necessity* of going to

[5] *Suppl.*, q. 8, a. 5, ad 6.

Communion—and this is seldom verified. To illustrate it we might reconsider three of the cases previously mentioned.

In the problem presented to Father O'Donnell the questioner apparently had no opportunity of going to confession, but his only reason for going to Communion was that he "wanted to receive Our Blessed Lord the following morning." This desire, though it may be very strong and is very laudable, does not make Communion a necessity. There is a necessity of going to Communion only when abstinence from Communion would be accompanied by some very extraordinary inconvenience.

Another case is that of the person who is already kneeling at the Communion rail when he realizes that he should have gone to confession. Clearly, as we pointed out, confession is now impossible; and, if he cannot leave the rail without exposing himself to suspicion, there is also a necessity of communicating —that is, abstinence from Communion would be accomplished by the extraordinary inconvenience of danger to his reputation. Granted that this circumstance existed, he could legitimately receive Communion after having made an act of perfect contrition.

A third example was taken from Father Healy's *Christian Guidance*. Since Father Healy uses this particular example primarily to illustrate a necessity of communicating, it may be helpful to quote it in its entirety:

> It has been the custom for some years that the whole Baxter family receive Holy Communion on De-

cember 12, the day on which Mrs. Baxter died. Mr. Baxter had received Holy Communion the day before at the Sunday Mass and now he comes to church with his grown children. Unfortunately, he committed a serious sin the previous afternoon, and he is counting on going to confession before Mass. However, when Baxter arrives he finds that Father Treacy, the only priest at this church, has already begun the prayers at the foot of the altar. Baxter cannot pretend that he violated the Eucharistic fast, for his children know that he did not. He cannot feign sickness, for he is obviously in the best of health. Unless he receives Holy Communion, his family will conclude that he is in the state of mortal sin.

Father Healy comments: "Given these circumstances, Mr. Baxter may make an act of perfect contrition and licitly go to Holy Communion at this Mass." I believe that theologians would generally agree with this solution because the circumstances all build up to an entirely exceptional situation—a situation which not only excludes the possibilty of confession but also makes abstinence from Communion a source of extraordinary inconvenience. And if the case were changed so that the children were young, instead of grown-up, there might be the added factor of danger of bad example if the father were to abstain from Communion in the circumstance described. A case in which similar circumstances might prevail would be a wedding, when the bride and the groom had planned on receiving Communion together at the Nuptial Mass.

It may be taken as a sound working principle that if abstinence from Communion would jeopardize one's reputation or give bad example, then Communion is necessary, in the sense of canon 856. But as I suggested with reference to confession, it is easier to enunciate a principle like this than to judge its practical application. It is sometimes said, for instance, that these inconveniences are apt to exist in a convent, or when sisters go to Communion daily in the parish church, or when they receive Communion with the children on special occasions, such as First Fridays. We are dealing here with a question of fact, and I certainly would not want to be dogmatic in affirming or denying the existence of the conditions. *If* they exist, they constitute a necessity of communicating. But clearly the Church does not want them to exist; and there is no valid reason why they should exist, because occasional abstinence from Communion is certainly not a sound basis for either suspicion or scandal.

All theologians say that the mere desire to receive Communion does not make Communion a necessity. In other words, the sorrow felt by a devout person who is deprived of Communion is not an extraordinary inconvenience in the sense of canon 856. This is undoubtedly true when the omission of Communion would be required for only a day or two. But I think there is room for an easier judgment in the case of a devout daily communicant, especially a religious, who might have to omit Communion for a rather long time. I am thinking particularly of an earnest religious who might very rarely commit a serious sin and who on one of these rare occasions might be in circumstances in which confession would be impossible for a week or so. I believe that abstinence from Communion during all that time would constitute an extraordinary hardship for such a religious—a hardship of such an exceptional nature as to constitute a justification for receiving Holy Communion after regaining grace through perfect contrition. This case is admittedly rare; but it can happen, especially in some rural districts.

Throughout this present section I have tried to stress two points: first, that the combination of circumstances demanded by the latter part of canon 856 should be seldom verified; and secondly, that it can be verified occasionally, even in the case of religious. But whenever a religious finds that these exceptions are frequent, there is something radically wrong—a situation which should not exist and which must be corrected. In this regard, I should like to refer to a question once answered in *Review for Religious* [6] concerning a young sister with a problem that called for frequent confession. She was in a place where such frequent confession was practically impossible and she thought that "frequent abstaining from Communion, especially as this might often be for several days at a time, would enable others to suspect her trouble." I believe that the answer we published at that time bears repetition here:

> It is not easy to answer a problem like this in a few words; but we can give a general idea of the points that must be considered. An occasional emergency when Communion is judged necessary and confession is impossible is understandable and might occur in the

[6] V (1946), 70-71.

life of almost anyone. But a state of affairs that makes such emergencies more or less habitual ought to be remedied. In the case referred to in the question, the religious should ask for a change of residence that would enable her to confess when necessary and to *obtain competent direction* concerning her problem. If she cannot bring herself to ask for the change and is unable to clear up the problem, she ought seriously to consider whether she has the requisite qualities for leading the religious life. Decisions like this ought to be made while religious are still young. If some problems are not faced and settled in the early years of the religious life they can eventually reach a point where a satisfactory solution is practically impossible.

The change of residence suggested in this answer can hardly be made judiciously unless the superior is given some information as to the nature of the problem.[7] Humility, therefore, is a requisite for the religious; but, needless to say, a religious who is unwilling to practice such humility when salvation itself might be concerned has lost his sense of values. On the other hand, the superior should be approachable, sympathetic, and very careful to observe strict secrecy.

IV. PRECAUTIONS TO BE TAKEN TO AVOID THE UNNECESSARY USE OF EXCEPTIONS TO THE ORDINARY LAW OF CONFESSION BEFORE COMMUNION AND TO GUARD AGAINST SACRILEGIOUS COMMUNIONS

Under date of December 8, 1938, the Sacred Congregation of the Sacraments issued an instruction for

7 Cf. *Review for Religious*, VI (1947), 242-247.

local ordinaries and major religious superiors which called attention to the fact that frequency of Communion could lead to diminished esteem for the Blessed Sacrament and that reception in groups could lead to sacrilegious Communions. The purpose of the instruction was to outline a number of steps to be taken to preclude these evils. There is a complete English version of this instruction in *Canon Law Digest* (II, 208-215) and an outline of it in *Review for Religious* (III, 268-270). The same number of the *Review* (pp. 252-267) carries a commentary on the instruction by Father Émile Bergh, S.J., together with some notes by the editors and some references to other commentaries. Since these various references cover the matter completely, I shall conclude the present article with only brief references to some of the main precautions.

The first precaution is to give proper doctrinal and ascetical instruction regarding the Holy Eucharist. This kind of instruction should engender a profound esteem for the Blessed Sacrament, a desire to communicate frequently and worthily, and a wholesome abhorrence of sacrilege. Through such instruction one would see that daily Communion is a great privilege, but not a necessity. Moreover, though Communion is not reserved to the saints, it does suppose a minimum disposition of freedom from mortal sin, and nothing justifies its conscious reception in this state. And although one need not have the most perfect motive, such as disinterested love of God, one should have a supernatural motive, such as the desire to avoid sin, preserve grace, grow in grace, and so on.

Should instruction be given, not only about the

necessity of regaining grace through confession, but also about the exception which permits the reception of Communion with only an act of perfect contrition? If one were to judge from some of the religious texts I have seen, one would conclude that the faithful are to be told only about the necessity of confession, and nothing about the exceptions mentioned in canon 856. This does not seem fair. If the faithful are obliged to keep a law, they are entitled to know what the law means, how seriously it obliges, and what are at least the more common legitimate exceptions. I admit that this has to be adapted to the age of the people concerned. Yet surely even a child can be taught that if he commits a mortal sin he should go to confession before receiving Communion; but that if he cannot avoid going to Communion and cannot get to confession, then he should make an act of perfect contrition before Communion. He might also be told that if ever he should have to do this, it would be well for him to explain the case in his next confession and see whether the confessor would want to give him some advice for the future.

A second precaution is to provide ample opportunity for confession before Communion. For religious in particular this means safeguarding the liberty of confession as granted in the canons; and for parishes, schools, institutions, and religious houses, it means that whenever it is feasible a confessor should be available before Mass. This latter provision should certainly be very helpful in larger convents, but I do not clearly see how it would be either convenient or effective in some very small convents.

A third precaution is to avoid practices that make

it difficult for individuals to abstain from Communion. It is ordinarily not prudent, for instance, for a teacher to say to a pupil, or a superior to a subject: "What's the matter—are you ill? I noticed you didn't go to Communion this morning." Also, if a "general" Communion is had, it should be done in such a way that no one feels obliged to go or that no attention will be called to those who do not go. So, too, prizes are not to be given for frequent Communion, and contests that highlight the reception of Communion by individuals should not be held.

As regards circumstances that make it difficult to abstain from Communion, the instruction, referring especially to the effect of these things on young people, said there should be "no rigid and quasi-military order in coming up, no insignia to be worn by those who receive Communion, etc." Some commentators have inferred from this that communities of religious women ought to abandon their custom of approaching the Communion rail in a certain order. Some have put this rather strongly, as if the instruction demanded it. One of the milder comments runs as follows: "It would certainly be praiseworthy and according to the spirit of the Instruction if the rigid and almost sacrosanct order of approaching the communion rails (Mother Superior, the Assistant, the senior nuns, etc.) were abolished; in convents human respect may do more mischief than in men's communities."

No doubt, good might come from dropping the order of precedence; but I do not share the great enthusiasm of some writers about its possible good effects. For one thing, a large number of our religious are in small communities, where abstaining from Communion would be noticeable no matter what order or lack of order prevailed. Even as regards larger communities, I wonder how long it would take, after the prescribed order of precedence had been dropped, for the religious to establish their own order. Most of us are confirmed routinists. Give a community enough time—and I doubt whether much time would be required—and one would note that the same ones go to Communion first, the same ones go last, and of course the same ones are in the middle. Perhaps I am wrong. But if I am right, then the best precaution is, not in the mechanics of going to Communion, but in the general cultivation of a mental attitude which allows everyone liberty of spirit, both in going to confession and in abstaining from Communion.

PART IV

Guidance by Religious

From a cursory glance at the chapter titles of this section, one might conclude that they deal with a variety of disconnected topics. Nevertheless, miscellaneous though they are, the topics were chosen because they represent some of the main ideas that must be kept in mind by a religious who gives spiritual advice to the laity. Except for the first, which gives a general picture of the requisites for such guidance, each of the chapters treats a specific problem that any counselor might have to face and for which he ought to have a clear answer.

chapter 10

Qualities of a Good
Moral Guide

I WAS once asked to give a conference to religious and lead a discussion on the qualities of a good moral guide. In preparing the conference I was impressed by the fact that among Catholics the most important of all moral guides is the confessor, and that all who give extra-confessional moral guidance must possess, to some degree at least, the personal qualifications which the Church expects her confessors to have. It seemed quite logical and practical, therefore, to base the conference on the qualities of a good confessor enumerated in the *Roman Ritual,* and to explain them in much the same way as moral theologians explain them when treating of the minister of the sacrament of penance. That is the plan I followed in the conference, and that is the plan I shall follow here. But, before discussing the qualities of a good moral guide, it seems advisable to determine what is meant by moral guidance and who might reasonably be considered as moral guides.

A "guide" points the way to something, helps others to attain a goal of some kind. A "moral" guide

—that is, a guide in *moral* matters—is one who helps others to lead good lives and thus to achieve the best and highest of goals, their salvation and sanctification. Such, I think, is the accepted meaning of moral guidance in the Catholic Church: guidance in things that pertain to *virtuous* living.

Very likely, when we think of guidance, we usually think of it in terms of direction given to individuals— by confessors, for example, spiritual directors, and student counselors. Yet it would be a mistake to limit the meaning to such formal, individual relationships. The teacher who explains the commandments of God, the precepts of the Church, or the evangelical counsels, is certainly giving moral guidance, not to an individual, it is true, but to an entire group. So, too, the teacher who in an informal way answers the questions concerning right conduct that students are wont to ask after class hours is really giving moral guidance, even though not in the official capacity of a student counselor.

From what I have said, it is clear that the term "moral guide" is applicable to a wide range of persons: parents, teachers, youth counselors, religious superiors, spiritual directors of religious, confessors, and all others who, in at least an informal and general way, give advice on moral matters. In a class by himself is the confessor, because of his unique power of absolving and because, quite naturally, certain problems will be referred to him which will rarely, if ever, be referred to the others. However, if we exclude what belongs uniquely to the confessor, it is apparent that all the other moral guides I have mentioned share with him to some degree the office of directing souls and should therefore be proportionately endowed with the qualities the Church expects him to possess. The remaining sections of this chapter are based on this assumption. I might add, however, that in drawing the parallel between the confessor and extra-confessional moral guides I have particularly in mind those religious who have been entrusted with the special office of guiding youth—student counselors, for instance.

The *Ritual* lays stress on these four qualities of a good confessor: knowledge, prudence, holiness, and a careful observance of secrecy. It would be difficult, if not impossible, to think of a more apt and adequate summary of qualifications for good moral guidance, whether in or out of the confessional.[1]

Knowledge

That those who guide others in the way of salvation must have *some* knowledge seems too obvious to need comment. The blind cannot lead the blind. Yet, it is distressing to note how often one hears remarks like these: "You don't need knowledge; all you need is common sense. . . . In the guidance of youth, and especially of children, common sense and sound piety will take care of everything." Such statements are sheer nonsense. Common sense and sound piety cer-

1 The material given here is developed more completely in *The Good Confessor* (New York: Sentinel Press, 1951). Although this little book was written for confessors, religious counselors could undoubtedly profit by reading it. In fact, the late Canon E. J. Mahoney recommended that the educated laity read it in order to get a better understanding of the function of a confessor.

tainly have their places in moral guidance, as will be explained later; but they will not supply for a lack of knowledge of God's laws and of the teaching and laws of the Church. Nor will they supply the factual knowledge of such things as physiology and psychology that is sometimes required for appropriate guidance.

It is one thing to say that guidance presupposes knowledge, and quite another to say just what the moral guide should know and how much he should know. The basic studies that enter into the training of a confessor are moral theology, canon law, and ascetical theology. Besides these, it is presupposed that as a priest he will know dogmatic theology. I think it is safe to say that these same subjects should form the basis for extra-confessional guidance. The required essential knowledge would differ, therefore, rather in degree than in kind. All guides should know at least the laws of the Church that ordinary Catholics must observe and the approved explanations of these laws. They should also know the main principles of Catholic morality and asceticism.

Guides deal with human beings; they must therefore know something of that highly interesting thing sometimes referred to as "human nature." Though a great deal of knowledge about human nature can be gleaned from personal experience and close observation of one's own and others' reactions, personal experience is not ordinarily sufficient for the moral guide; he should also know something of the excellent scientific studies now available on child psychology, adolescent psychology, the psychology of character, mental hygiene, and so forth. In reading such works, however, the moral guide may himself need the guidance of a competent psychologist; for, besides the excellent material written on these subjects, there is no small amount of unreliable and even basically unchristian material.

How much must one know in order to give proper guidance? The only answer is that it depends on the kind of guidance one is expected to give. The usual norm for the minimum amount of knowledge of moral theology required of a confessor is this: he should know enough to solve the ordinary cases likely to be presented to him in the place where he is to hear confessions and should be able to recognize exceptionally difficult cases that demand further study or consultation with experts. I believe that same norm may be applied proportionately to all guides, and I doubt whether anything more definite can be given in a general treatment like this.

Prudence

Prudence is the virtue which "helps us in all circumstances to form a right judgment as to what we should seek or avoid for the sake of eternal life." [2] When we speak of this virtue with regard to a director of souls, the "eternal life" that we have principally in mind is not the spiritual good of the director but rather the good of the person he is directing. In other words, the spiritual guide must judge what is conducive, or more conducive, to the salvation and

2 See Peter Cardinal Gasparri: *Catholic Catechism* (New York: Kenedy, 1932).

sanctification of his charge and then give his counsel accordingly.

It is not correct, however, to say that the spiritual director seeks *only* the good of the persons he is directing. True prudence must take in the whole picture. One is not prudent who harms his own soul in trying to benefit others. Nor is one prudent who seeks to help an individual at the expense of a greater good—for example, the good of the whole community, or the good of the whole Church. An adequate description of the prudent guide would, therefore, be stated somewhat as follows: he is one who uses his knowledge, his personality, and his influence on others in such a way as to attain the good of the soul he is directing without at the same time harming his own soul or defeating a greater good. In fact, when correctly interpreted, the words *ad majorem Dei gloriam* formulate a perfect rule of prudence.

Without further theorizing on this virtue, I should like to state a number of practical points concerning the exercise of prudence in giving moral guidance. I am listing these points more or less in the style of jottings because the subject is too large for more complete treatment here; and, though I generally dislike negatives, I think it will be especially convenient to put these suggestions in the form of a series of *don'ts*. Some of these *don'ts* may appear to be more directly concerned with the technique of counseling than with the virtue of prudence; yet, as I have already indicated, the actual exercise of prudence consists not only in directing souls towards a certain end but also in choosing the most appropriate means for attaining this end, and technique (or tact) is a very important means in the direction of others.

Don't scold. Even people who ask for a scolding do not usually want it and are rather alienated than helped by it. I still remember a story told during one of my novitiate retreats which aptly illustrates this point. In a certain parish there was a very devout woman who yearned to scale the heights of holiness. Having heard that trials and humiliations are essential for this, she pleaded insistently with her pastor, "Try me, Father. Please, try me, Father." The pastor was a peace-loving man and had no inclination to accede to her desires; but one day when she returned some altar linens she had laundered, he kept her for a few minutes and began examining the linens in her presence. As he looked at each piece he called attention to some imaginary (or real) defect in the laundering. A few minutes of this was all that the would-be saint could endure. She burst into tears and began to upbraid the pastor for his ingratitude. But he cut her short in the midst of her tirade with a dry smile and the chiding rebuke, "Try me, Father. Please, try me, Father."

Don't interrupt unnecessarily. It is generally better for the guide to allow his consultant to tell his entire story and then ask questions about points that need further elucidation. Unnecessary interruptions may cause confusion and even irritation. Moreover, they can easily impede the perfect spontaneity of the narrative and result in a "coloring" of the story according to some preconceived notion of the director.

Don't make yourself indispensable to your con-

sultants. Even children should gradually be emancipated from the need of obtaining advice about the ordinary moral problems of life. And, though maturity does not entirely relieve one of this need, yet progress towards maturity should markedly diminish the need of seeking advice in ordinary matters. The best type of spiritual direction consists in helping one to do his own planning—with the help of the Holy Ghost, of course; and the guidance of even the immature and the mentally unsettled should be directed towards this same end.

Don't unnecessarily send consultants to someone else. Boys and girls sometimes ask their teachers about their problems because they have confidence in these teachers. It is not prudent to send them elsewhere, even to a confessor, if one can easily solve the problem, for they usually accept help most willingly from those in whom they can readily confide. And this is also true of adults.

The opposite of this error should also be avoided: that is, counselors should never show resentment if their consultants wish to seek guidance from someone else. In this matter one should keep in mind the liberty that the Church extends to the faithful regarding the choice of confessors. The same liberty should be enjoyed by those who seek extra-confessional guidance. *Feelings* of superiority or of jealousy, even among those who work for God, are quite human and excusable; but the deliberate yielding to and manifestation of such feelings by bragging or criticism is petty and can do great harm to God's cause.

Don't destroy confidence in others. I am thinking of cases such as this: A priest sometimes finds that a child has a false notion of what is right or wrong because of something his mother told him or something a sister said. In correcting this erroneous conscience it is the priest's duty to try to do so in such a way as to preserve the child's confidence in his mother or the sister. He can usually do that by saying, "Your mother meant something like this . . ."; or, "The sister probably didn't mean it just that way." As a matter of fact, the child may have misunderstood his mother or the sister; but, even if he did not misunderstand, the priest should avoid giving the impression that the mother or the sister was wrong.

This case is merely an example. Anyone entrusted with the guidance of others can make a mistake, inculcate erroneous ideas, and foster a false conscience. Yet among all guides—whether parents, teachers, counselors, or confessors—there should be a spirit of what I might call "professional loyalty" which should prompt each one to correct the mistakes made by others without at the same time saying that they were mistakes. It is important for all of us that those who need guidance should retain their confidence in and respect for those who guide them.

Don't be too quick to solve problems that involve absent persons. When two parties are involved in a quarrel or a misunderstanding there are always two sides to the matter. If the consultant is one of the parties, he will very likely be prejudiced, even though he does not wish to be and sincerely thinks that he is not. In such cases the *ideal* solution is to get the two

[213]

parties together and then to thresh out the matter; but, of course, this may seldom be possible when a matter of conscience is involved. Nevertheless, even when the other party cannot be seen or interviewed, the guide should try to understand his side of the case before planning a course of action for his consultant.

Don't exaggerate the sex problem. Speaking of the confessor's prudence, moral theologians lay particular stress on the need of this virtue in all matters pertaining to sex. The theological axiom, "It is better to say too little than too much," applies not only to confessors but to all moral guides. Teachers and counselors need not be surprised if they find the topic interesting; yet they should not allow their interest to become morbid. They should not probe for sex problems, particularly for details concerning them. A probing tendency easily becomes morbid and often results in the ridicule of the teacher or counselor who manifests such a tendency. If a few students once suspect that a certain teacher or adviser is especially interested in sex problems, they will speedily pass the word on to others, and offensive nicknames will probably be coined.

I am not arguing for a Victorian silence concerning sex. I believe that the topic should be treated with a simple wholesomeness, but as *one part* of life, and not as the whole of life. The director who overemphasizes the subject will but defeat his own cause —and this, for one in the apostolic life, is a gross violation of the most fundamental rule of prudence. There are people—boys and girls, men and women—

even in this sex-conscious world of ours, who have absolutely no problem with regard to sex. It is very imprudent for a guide to create problems for such people by unnecessary questioning or by imparting useless information.

The Holy See has repeatedly called attention to the need of prudence, not only in treating the topic of sex, but also in dealing with the members of the opposite sex. Here again, I might mention that special interest is not unusual. It is certainly quite natural for a man to experience a special interest in associating with women; quite natural too that women will be particularly enthusiastic in helping boys and young men. To some extent this natural attractiveness can be made a powerful force in the spiritual life. But not if it gets out of control. The counselor who makes himself or herself a special apostle to the other sex is not likely to have the dignity, reserve, and purity of intention required for true success. Hence, while on the one hand it is not right for anyone to cultivate an attitude of disdain for the other sex and to become a man-hater or a woman-hater, it is nevertheless necessary to avoid the other extreme of giving the impression that one's life is divinely dedicated only to the opposite sex. Furthermore, one must remember that even innocent relationships can appear unsavory and thus harm the cause of Christ.

Don't give information that can't be digested. Those who teach and advise children are particularly in need of this caution. Children cannot assimilate all the fine distinctions one learns in ethics and in moral theology: for example, the teaching on mental reservation, the cases involving the "double effect," the difference between the absolute and the relative methods of calculating grave sins of theft. We can safely say that children should never be told what is false; but it does not follow from this that they should always be told the *whole* truth. For instance, children should be correctly instructed as to what to do when they doubt whether they have broken the Eucharistic fast, whether they have yielded to a serious temptation, whether they are excused from hearing Mass, and so forth; and from the solutions of these individual problems they will gradually learn by induction the very important principles regarding the solution of the so-called "doubtful conscience." The same is true of other moral and ascetical principles. Children learn them best through concrete examples and through the solution of individual cases, since they are hardly capable of learning the principle first and then applying it to practical cases. But the teacher or the director must know the principle well; otherwise he might cause confusion in making the transition from one case to another.

Don't guess an answer. If I had to grade errors in prudence according to their potential harmfulness, I would put this among the most serious. If the director does not know the answer to a question or the solution to a problem, he should say so. It is the common experience, even of those who teach children, that omniscience is not expected of human beings and that the sincere admission of ignorance does not undermine confidence. On the other hand, it is evident that great harm can result from trying to solve vital problems by guesswork.

Some go to the opposite extreme in this matter: they never give a definite answer, even when they are reasonably certain about the correct solution. This type of guide has the same attitude toward his consultants' problems that the scrupulous person entertains towards his own. The latter is always *afraid* he is wrong; and he finds it difficult, if not impossible, to make himself follow what are in themselves perfectly reasonable judgments. Similarly, the timorous guide will not trust his own judgment and will fear to commit himself in the solution of practical moral problems. In other words, he is no guide at all.

Don't fret over errors made in good faith. It is very helpful for those who direct consciences to examine themselves periodically in order to see how they ask questions, solve problems, deal with different personalities, and so on. If this is done calmly and solely with a view to self-improvement, it is a salutary and commendable practice; but if it becomes an occasion of generating worries, it is useless and even harmful. It can make the office of guiding others an intolerable burden. None of us is infallible except the pope; and his infallibility is circumscribed by many conditions.

Holiness

Some years ago I read an instructive incident from the life of Garcia Moreno, once President of Ecuador. If I remember the story correctly, it went somewhat like this. As a young man, Moreno was a master at explaining his Faith, but only a tyro at practicing it. One evening, in the course of a long discussion with a rationalist acquaintance, Moreno repeatedly got

[217]

the better of the arguments, and the rationalist finally admitted: "Everything you say seems to be true; yet I can't accept any of it, for your own life gives the lie to it all."

This story illustrates one reason why the wisest guidance is liable to be useless unless the guide is a person of solid virtue. Example speaks louder than words. This is particularly true of the young. They are very human; and it is but human to lose confidence in one who does not practice what he preaches, to balk at accepting high ideals from one who apparently has low personal ideals, to refuse to be taught honesty, purity, sobriety, and such virtues by one whose own life is not marked by them.

In fact, if we consider only good example, it seems that the extra-confessional guide is more in need of solid virtue than is the confessor; for the faithful in general are schooled in the principle that the sacraments do not depend on the holiness of the minister for their efficacy. Now, this principle does not hold for non-sacramental ministries. Hence, in one sense at least, the third requisite mentioned by the *Ritual* —"goodness of life"—pertains even more to the extra-sacramental guide than to the confessor.

It seems obvious that, quite apart from the need of confirming one's words by good example, the successful carrying on of moral guidance calls for the practice of many virtues. I will not try to enumerate them here, for I think that is unnecessary. The required virtues can be epitomized in one: charity— charity towards God and charity towards the neighbor.

Love of God is essential, since the direction of souls is His work and it must be unequivocally consecrated to Him. Some guides apparently have great success, even though they seem to be impelled mostly by a natural love for the work and by the natural satisfaction they obtain from having others depend on them, confide in them, and flatter them. This may seem so, but I wonder whether it actually is. Though God *can* no doubt work wonders with cheap instruments, it is hardly according to His ordinary providence to do so. Normally He works His marvels of grace through the instrumentality of those who are closely joined to Him by love.

Charity towards the neighbor is also necessary. The guide needs it first and foremost to give him a vital supernatural motivation. For even though it be true that some can be carried forward in this work by a natural liking—because they enjoy dealing with people or engaging in external occupations—this is by no means universally true. Most of those who are assigned to guidance work find that many who need their help are not naturally attractive. The guide needs to see these and all souls with the eyes of Christ; he has to realize that these souls who come to him for help are Christ's "least brethren"; that they were redeemed by the Blood of Christ; that they belong, or should belong, to the Mystical Body of Christ. Motivation on some lower plane easily springs from or degenerates into sheer selfishness, which uses guidance only as a means of self-expression and self-glorification—a sterile thing in the propagation of the Kingdom of God.

[219]

Charity towards the neighbor is not merely a motive force in guidance, it is also a supernatural tool that must be used constantly. In this regard I can think of nothing more appropriate than St. Paul's sublime eulogy: "Charity is patient, is kind; charity envieth not, dealeth not perversely, is not puffed up, is not ambitious, seeketh not her own, is not provoked to anger, thinketh no evil, rejoiceth not in iniquity, but rejoiceth with the truth: beareth all things, hopeth all things, endureth all things."

These inspired words merit constant meditation by the spiritual guide. But we shall have to leave them for meditation. I can only say a few words here about the first two qualities: "Charity is patient, is kind."

The ideal for all spiritual guides is, of course, our Lord Himself. Among the fruits of meditation on His life should be a sympathetic attitude towards others and an eagerness to help them, a desire to see the good in them and draw it to the surface, a readiness for the little courtesies and kindnesses that mean so much to the human heart. After all, if these little things mean much in ordinary life, they must mean even more to those who are seeking guidance and who are often nervous, despondent, and even frightened.

As for patience, the spiritual guide has countless occasions to practice it. Consultants are sometimes unpleasant in their manner; they fail to cooperate; they come at inconvenient times; they dwell lengthily on irrelevant trivialities; they occasionally manifest a gross selfishness by needlessly consuming time, as if under the impression that the guide has nothing to do but listen to them. Such things are liable to test patience to the breaking point. And then there is always the possibility of impatience with one's own self—that is, with one's inability to handle a case.

Some theologians advise priests to leave the confessional for a while when they find that they are becoming irritable, to walk for a few minutes in the fresh air, or to relax for a short time in the rectory. It is better to keep the people waiting for a little while than to run the risk of being sharp or rude. Similar advice may be profitable to all counselors. If one feels so ill-disposed that he cannot trust himself, it is better to avoid an interview or at least to keep it short and continue it later.

Secrecy

The fourth requisite for good spiritual guidance is respect for confidences. Religious, perhaps more than any others, should realize the importance of this qualification. They know the great peace and sense of security of individuals and of communities when superiors and directors are careful about respecting confidences, and they know what evils can result from the mere suspicion that someone in authority uses confidential information too freely.

Only the sacramental secret is absolutely inviolable. Other secrets admit at least theoretical and rare exceptions. But it is safe to say that in actual practice the spiritual guide should have a similar ideal with regard to secrecy that the Church constantly puts before her confessors. This ideal is succinctly proposed by St. Augustine as follows: "I know less about what

I hear in confession than I know about those things about which I know nothing."

Much more could be said about the obligation of secrecy, but I believe that for our present purpose it is sufficient to call attention to its importance. It puts what one might call the "finishing touch" on all the other qualities. If a director of souls lacks this quality, the others (even if possessed) will be useless; for the person who does not feel sure that his confidences will be respected simply will not seek guidance. On the other hand, if the director possesses this and the other qualities explained in the present chapter and uses them for the good of souls, he will accomplish great things for God and will earn for himself the reward promised to those who instruct others unto justice.

11

Vocational Counseling

ONE summer I had the enjoyable experience of leading a group of sisters in a course entitled Christian Vocations. In the class were thirty-six sisters, representing a variety of religious institutes. I designedly say I led them, rather than taught them, for when we began the course I had only a few germinal ideas and some scattered notes and references for developing the ideas. The actual development was carried out as a cooperative venture, with the class contributing as much as the teacher. At the conclusion of the course we were all satisfied, I think, that we had really something substantial and that the process of achievement had been anything but dull.

I believe that some of the main points discussed in our class would be of interest and profit to other religious, since most of them are engaged, at least occasionally and informally, in vocational counseling. And even if they are not, they feel a natural interest in the subject of vocations, and their personal attitudes towards it can scarcely fail to influence their own lives and the lives of others. These attitudes may receive some benefit from the points to be treated here. I might add that these points are not intended as a complete development of the theme of vocational counseling; they are merely notes on some of its more important aspects.

Meaning of "Vocation"

What is a vocation? Theologically, this term can have a wide variety of meanings, as is ably shown by Monsignor William R. O'Connor in *The Layman's Call*.[1] In our class we considered two meanings, one primary, the other secondary.

In its primary meaning vocation may be defined as "a divine call to embrace a definite state of life." In general, the Christian states of life are two: marriage and virginity. The latter may take any one of several forms: the priesthood, the religious life, and virginity in the world. Moreover, the priesthood itself may be subdivided into diocesan and regular. Hence, there are really five basic states of life [2] that may be the objects of a divine call; and it is imperative that a vocational counselor take cognizance of and appreciate them all. This may require considerable effort at mental readjustment and great care in the use of the word "vocation," for undoubtedly most of us religious, if not all (and the laity, too), have become accustomed to think of vocation as synonymous with *religious* vocation—that is, with the call to the priesthood or to the religious life.

This readjustment must be made, first, because the

[1] New York: Kenedy, 1942.

[2] Even this division is perhaps not technically adequate, because it does not make sufficient provision for vocations to institutes that lead a community life but do not take public vows (cf. canons 673-81) or to secular institutes.

narrower meaning is simply not correct. As Monsignor O'Connor points out, the Church is careful to qualify the term: for example, in the Code of Canon Law, by speaking of the *ecclesiastical* vocation, and, in the encyclical on Christian Education, of the *religious* and *priestly* vocations. And Pope Pius XII, in his address to Italian Women (October 21, 1945), speaking of women who because of the tragedies of the war were unable to marry, referred to their providential state (of enforced, or inevitable virginity in the world) as a divine vocation. I am not sure whether any ecclesiastical documents refer explicitly to marriage as a divine vocation, but certainly the notion is at least implied in the inspiring tone that pervades the encyclical of Pope Pius XI.

Theological accuracy, therefore, requires that counselors keep this broad notion of vocation, even in its primary sense. A further reason for preserving this breadth in our attitudes and our speech is that it increases the apostolic value of our dealings with youth. For youth, even those who consult us specifically about a religious vocation, like to see that we have an exalted notion of other states of life, and as a result of this they more willingly give us their confidence. As for marriage, in particular, if we are to accomplish the mission of bringing young men and women to a realization of the sacredness of family life, we must train them to embrace the married state and to persevere in it with the same desire to do God's will that should characterize the choice of and perseverance in the priesthood and the religious state.

A secondary meaning of vocation is "a divine call

to do a definite work"—for example, to teach, to be a missionary, to carry out a certain form of Catholic activity, to be a musician, and so forth. Monsignor O'Connor develops at great length the idea that such things are the objects of a divine vocation. A vocation, in this sense of the word, is usually subordinate to the more general call to a state of life, and sometimes it is merely what is termed an avocation.

In our class we limited ourselves for the most part, though not entirely, to the primary meaning of vocation; and that is what I shall do in these notes. It should not be inferred from this, however, that the secondary meaning of vocation is lacking in importance. As a matter of fact, for each individual his *complete* vocation (that is, the complete plan of God for him) embraces not only his state of life but also the work that he is to do in that state, as well as the degree of perfection he is to attain in that state and work; and not infrequently individuals discover God's will in regard to their state of life because they can easily recognize His will concerning the work they are to do.

God's Will

Since vocation is a divine call, it follows that those who wish to make a correct choice of their vocation must be willing to listen to God; in other words, they must have a sincere desire to know and do His will. When they actually make a choice, they should do so, not precisely because of their own likes or dislikes, or their own preferences or prejudices, but rather because they are honestly convinced that this is what

God wants them to do. Applying this literally, it means that even those who enter marriage should do so because they believe that God is calling them to that state of life. No doubt this sounds quite idealistic, for it seems that very few of those who marry do so with any consciousness of a divine call. In fact, as regards marriage, they are simply not vocation-conscious. It is for us to bring them to this consciousness; and it can be done, at least in a large number of cases, if the vocational aspect of marriage is given sufficient emphasis by teachers and other guides of youth.

Failure to cultivate the disposition of placing God's will first and of making one's choice of vocation according to that norm is not limited to the married. Many who enter seminaries and novitiates do so without sufficient consideration of the divine will and with too much consideration of their own likes or, as they say, their own "happiness"—by which they too often mean "earthly happiness." No doubt it would be unrealistic to expect them to make this choice only on the basis of a purely disinterested love of God; but at least they should be helped to make it with a proper understanding of their *true* happiness, and with an appropriate subordination of their feelings to the desire of pleasing God.

The counselor, too, must be devoted to God's will. In practice, religious counselors do not easily acquire or sustain this disposition. When we observe a "fine boy or girl" we almost spontaneously think, "He would make a wonderful priest—or brother" or "She would be a splendid sister," and we are very much inclined to rest in this decision and even to guide these fine boys and girls in the same direction without further thought of God's will. Yet, just as the young people must have the disposition of wanting to know and do God's will in whatever state of life He wishes, so must the counselor have the same detached objectivity.

The inclination to forestall God's will is perhaps even stronger when we are guiding someone who has decided to enter religion but has not determined what institute he should enter. We naturally think primarily in terms of our own institute—we know so much about it, are so attached to it and so deeply conscious of its needs. Yet here, too, the disposition of seeking only the will of God is a requisite for good counseling. Acquaintance with other religious institutes through association and reading is a help towards the desirable objectivity.

Obviously, I am not implying here that we should not inform boys and girls about the priesthood and the religious life, or that we should not make known our own spirit and our own needs. It is our duty to do such things and to foster religious vocations of all kinds. But in praying for and guiding any individual there must always be the condition "if God so wills."

A Plan of Study

Almighty God no doubt has many ways of manifesting His will to us. In the case of some saints He has even made use of private revelations for this purpose. But the ordinary way of discerning one's vocation in life includes the calm, reasonable answering of such questions as these: (1) What are my *oppor-*

tunities (or possibilities)? If the circumstances of one's life make it clear that only one of the basic states of life is possible for him (for example, because of illness), then it seems rather obvious that God is calling him to that state of life. On the other hand, if one has at least the opportunity of choosing between two or more states of life (as would usually be the case with the youth whom we guide), one must go on to the second question. (2) What are my *qualifications?* And here again, if one should find that one is really qualified for only one state of life, it seems that one may reasonably judge that God wishes him to embrace that state. However, if the individual finds that he is qualified for more than one, God's preference is not yet apparent, and a third question must be answered. (3) For which of these states of life am I *best qualified?* The presumption seems to be that God gives a true grace of vocation when by the light of His grace He enables an individual to judge: "I would best serve my own true interests, or best follow Christ, or best serve God, in this particular state of life." That is what I mean when I say "best qualified."

Counselors should be prepared to help others to answer these questions. The answer to the first question should rarely present serious difficulty. On the contrary, the third question may require the help of a highly trained and experienced spiritual director. But all counselors should be able to give some aid towards answering the second question, at least to the extent of outlining the required qualifications for each of the states of life. In our class, therefore, we emphasized the second question, and made it the basis of the major part of our course.

How does one determine the requisite qualities for the various states of life? One evident way (and perhaps the only way) is to study the duties of each state of life and the consequent demands that it is likely to make on those who embrace it. The logic of this method appealed to us, and we made it the basis for our plan of study: we would consider first the *duties* of each state of life, and then the *qualities* necessary for fulfilling these duties. (A third point might be added: namely, the *preparation* needed for acquiring the qualities.)

It is practically impossible to list the specific duties of the single life in the world; hence, in following our plan of studying the duties and the requisite qualities for the various states of life, we confined ourselves to the priesthood, marriage, and the religious life. Though we gave about equal time to each of these states, for the purpose of illustration I shall here outline only our procedure regarding the religious life.

The Religious Life

A prerequisite for entrance into religion is freedom from canonical impediments. The duties common to all religious include the observance of the vows, community life, and the regular practice of certain acts of piety. Besides these general duties, there are the specific duties of the various institutes. After discussing the implications of the various duties, and after considerable trial and error in the formulating of questions, we finally settled on five basic questions that a vocational counselor should use in helping a prospective candidate for the religious life. The questions, with some brief comments, are as follows:

1. *Is the candidate free from canonical impediments?* These impediments are enumerated in canon 542 and are explained by the canonists.[3] Besides these impediments of general law, particular institutes sometimes have further impediments established by their own constitutions. Obviously, a vocational counselor cannot be expected to know the special regulations of all the various institutes; but certainly he should know the impediments established by the Code of Canon Law and, if he is advising a person about a particular institute, he should try to learn something about the requirements of that institute.

It is worth noting here that the mere existence of an impediment does not necessarily mean the lack of vocation. Much depends on whether the impediment is removable, and how easily it is removable. For example, canon law does not make illegitimacy an impediment to the religious life; yet some institutes, especially of women, do make illegitimacy an impediment to entrance. It does not follow from this that a counselor should tell a girl who is illegitimate, but otherwise well qualified, that God is not calling her to one of these institutes. He should first prudently

3 See, for example, Abbo-Hannan, *The Sacred Canons* (St. Louis: Herder, 1952), I, 558-571; Bouscaren-Ellis, *Canon Law: A Text and Commentary* (Milwaukee: Bruce, 1955), pp. 260-263; J. Creusen, *Religious Men and Women in the Code* (Milwaukee: Bruce, 1953), pp. 129-134.

inquire whether the superiors of the institute want to accept her and to ask for a dispensation from the impediment. Bishops can grant this dispensation if the superiors wish it.

2. *Is the candidate emotionally mature?* For a study of emotional maturity see Chapter I. It seems safe to say that one who is sufficiently mature can successfully observe the vows of poverty and obedience, can put up with the hardships of community life, and has the moral stamina required for trying to advance in perfection. Very likely this broad statement will not be immediately apparent to those who read it, but I believe that those who weigh it carefully will agree with it. In our class we made lengthy lists of the qualities necessary for observing poverty, obedience, and so forth, but soon discovered that all these qualities should normally be found in the truly mature person.

3. *Can the candidate observe the obligation of celibacy without extraordinary difficulty?* It may be that the mature person is sufficiently master of his emotions to observe perfect chastity; but this is not clear to me, and I believe that the subject of chastity merits special consideration in any candidate for the religious life.

In this matter, both candidates and counselors must be careful to observe a fundamental principle of prudence: *Do not assume an obligation that you can fulfill only with extraordinary difficulty, unless there are very special indications that God wishes you to assume it.* This principle is universal, and it applies to all matters; but it has special reference to

the duty of celibacy. To assume extraordinarily difficult obligations without special reasons may be the
equivalent of exposing oneself unnecessarily to occasions of sin and even to the danger of giving great
scandal to others. It is definitely not wise to assume,
or to encourage others to assume, the duty of observing perfect chastity when one's past record or one's
temperament indicates that the fulfillment of this
duty is problematical.

To judge these matters one must know the individual, his record, and his temperament. This is one
reason why the advice of a confessor is often the deciding element in judging a religious vocation.
Teachers and other counselors should be very careful about pushing one who seems to be "a good boy
or a good girl" into religion, for they are frequently
quite unaware of the difficulties that make these
"good young people" hesitate. Of course, difficulty,
even great difficulty, is not in itself an obstacle to the
celibate vocation; but difficulty, combined with manifest weakness, or with inability to confide in a director, or with a lack of appreciation of the safeguards
to chastity, is certainly a sufficient reason to make
one hesitate about assuming or encouraging the assumption of this obligation. To tell one who has
given evidence of habitual weakness that it will "all
clear up in the novitiate" is the height of imprudence.
It may clear up in the novitiate, only to return with
even greater force later!

4. *Has the candidate the solid piety required for
leading a life in which the regular performance of
spiritual exercises plays a prominent part?* How does

one judge the presence or absence of this solid piety? In our classroom discussions we found it difficult to express any accurate norm. We all agreed, of course, that a likely candidate for the religious life need not (perhaps, should not?) be the eyes-down, hands-folded-over-breast, always-in-church type. But his life should give evidence of a sound appreciation of his religion by such features as frequent confession and Communion, the consistent use of prayer, and the willingness to aid in apostolic ventures. This must seem rather indefinite to the reader, yet it is the best we can do on this point.

5. *Can the candidate do some work that is done by at least one religious institute, active or contemplative?* "Work" in this question has a wide meaning; it includes apostolic activities, intellectual pursuits, manual work, and prayer. The purpose of the question is to determine whether the candidate has the physical health and the talent which would make him acceptable to one or more of the various religious institutes.

To close this section, let me say that the questions just listed and briefly explained are the result of our study of the *duties* of the religious state and of the *qualities* required for entrance. A negative answer to any of the questions would mean that the candidate does not have a vocation to the religious life—at least not yet. An affirmative answer, on the other hand, would not immediately point to such a vocation; for it may be that the candidate is even better qualified for some other state of life and that God prefers him to embrace this other state. And I might add, just for completeness, that even when the vocation to the religious state is clear, there is still the problem of deciding what institute one should enter.

Doubts

Before concluding these notes, I should like to return to the general topic of vocations and touch upon three important points. The first of these concerns *doubts*. Doubts about vocation can take a variety of forms; and, though we cannot treat them all here, we can refer to some of them. For instance, a young man or a young woman (or both) is hesitant about getting married; they keep putting it off because one or the other (or both) cannot make a decision. Or a young woman thinks she should enter religion, but she is not sure she has a vocation. These are typical cases. What should the counselor do about them? One thing a counselor should *not* do is make the decision for his consultant. A divine vocation is a grace or, perhaps better, a series of graces culminating in the light to know the divine will. It is a grace given to the individual, not to his counselor; and no decision of the counselor is a safe substitute for it.

The counselor's function, therefore, is to help the consultant clear up his own doubt. One way of doing this is to inquire into the reason for the doubt. It may be that the consultant is habitually indecisive, or habitually dependent on others for his decisions. If this is so, he seems to lack the maturity necessary for embracing a permanent state of life and should first acquire this maturity by learning to make decisions for himself. Or it may be that the "doubt" is rather a misunderstanding of the certainty required for a vocation. Some young men and women apparently think that an extraordinary degree of certainty is required for this decision: through their ignorance they look for an illumination that has the force of a private revelation. Their entire difficulty may clear up if it is pointed out to them that the grace of vocation may well be indicated in a quiet judgment to this effect: "As far as I can see, this—or that—state of life seems best for me." Finally, there is the case in which one has the requisite maturity, has prayed earnestly, has considered the matter reasonably, and is still unable to decide what he should do. Granted these conditions, it seems that he does not yet have a vocation to embrace some definite state of life, and a permanent decision should be postponed.

Role of Parents

The concluding section of the encyclical on Christian Marriage contains many wise directives for young men and women with regard to the choice of a partner for marriage. The last of these directives runs as follows:

> Lastly, let them not fail to ask the prudent advice of their parents with regard to the partner and let them regard this advice in no light manner, in order that by their mature knowledge and experience of human affairs they may guard against a baneful mistake, and on the threshold of matrimony may receive more abundantly the Divine blessing. . . .

In these words, the Holy Father clearly indicates the role of parents regarding the vocation of marriage: the parents are counselors and, all other things being equal, the first among counselors. But they are *only* counselors; they have no right to make the choice for their children or to force them to this or that choice. The Church insistently defends the right of the child to make his own choice of a state of life.

In regard to other states of life, parents also have a right to advise, insofar as they are capable. Their ability, however, is greatly limited because of their lack of knowledge of these other states. Nevertheless, with regard to religious and priestly vocations, they often assume powers that belong to no human being; they discourage such vocations and even blindly prevent them. It would be well if all would take to heart these other words of Pope Pius XI:

> Yet it must be confessed with sadness that only too often parents seem to be unable to resign themselves to the priestly or religious vocations of their children. Such parents have no scruple in opposing the Divine call with objections of all kinds; they even have recourse to means which can imperil not only the vocation to a more perfect state, but also the very conscience and the eternal salvation of those souls they ought to hold so dear. This happens all too often in the case even of parents who glory in being sincerely Christian and Catholic, especially in the higher and more cultured classes. This is a deplorable abuse, like that unfortunately prevalent in centuries past of forcing children into the ecclesiastical career without the fitness of a vocation. It hardly does honor to those higher classes of society, which are on the whole so scantily represented in the ranks of the clergy . . . . Did they indeed look at things in the light of faith, what greater dignity could Christian parents desire for their sons, what ministry more noble than that which, as We have said, is worthy of the veneration of men and angels? A long and sad experience has shown

that a vocation betrayed—the word is not to be thought too strong—is a source of tears not only for the sons but also for the ill-advised parents; and God grant that those tears be not so long delayed as to become eternal tears.

I have referred to this question of parental duty because in our capacity of counseling youth it is one of the most frequent vocational obstacles we must face. Parents impede good marriages and promote dangerous ones for what they call "social" reasons; they discourage talented boys from studying for the priesthood or from entering the religious life; and especially they make use of cunning or of moral pressure to keep their daughters out of convents. As teachers we must repeatedly give the true doctrine in a calm, objective way; and as counselors we must tactfully, but persistently, do what we can to see that it is followed. Many parents, thank God, are wonderfully cooperative; but not a few exaggerate their rights and are ignorant of their duties.

Prayer

In any study of vocations there is a danger of overemphasizing the mechanics of making decisions and of losing sight of the function of prayer. In concluding these notes, therefore, I wish to repeat that vocation is a grace, or a series of graces, and that it follows the law of distribution of graces. Hence, the one who is making the choice must pray; his advisers must pray; and all who are interested in a happy outcome must pray. Prayer for grace, and grace through prayer—that is the ordinary law of God's providence.

12

Moral Beauty in Our
Duties Towards God

In his treatise on the blessed Eucharist, St. Albertus
Magnus offers this humble apology for the limitations
of his work: "Even though we do the best we can,
yet in treating of God and the mysteries of God we
but babble like babes." In this respect, anyone who
tries to work out a scheme for the positive and in-
spirational treatment of the commandments that
enunciate our duties towards God will very likely
feel a certain kinship to the great Dominican scholar.
These commandments touch on sublime truths, "on
God and the mysteries of God," and it is difficult to
speak or write of these truths in words that offer
more than a glimmer of satisfaction.

Because of the difficulty of treating the subject
adequately, I prefer to consider the present chapter
merely a series of "notes" on our duties to God. The
ideas are not fully developed; but they do, I hope,
offer some material for that prayerful study of the
Decalogue, which, according to the Roman Catechism, is so desirable. Perhaps too, the general plan
given here will be of service to teachers who desire

material for presenting the positive background of the various commandments before explaining the precepts and prohibitions contained therein.

Reason and Faith

Our duties towards God are epitomized in the first three commandments of the Decalogue. These commandments, in turn, are summed up and perfected in the first of the two great commandments. In terms of the virtues, these commandments refer principally to acts of faith, hope, charity, and religion. The following notes will show, in a somewhat sketchy fashion, how the practice of these virtues is associated with the commandments, and will indicate, at least imperfectly, their power for contributing to the moral beauty of the universe.

Our duties toward God flow from definite relationships that exist between ourselves and God. The first step in the appreciation and observance of such duties must be a knowledge of these relationships. This knowledge is obtained through reason, and especially through faith. Even reason alone can tell us much about God and ourselves; from the visible things of this world, as St. Paul declared, it can penetrate to the invisible things of God. Reason can discover the existence of God and can paint a very sublime portrait of His perfections.

Nevertheless, much more important than mere reason is the knowledge that is ours through faith. In the first place, though reason can (perhaps I should say could) attain to a vast fund of knowledge about

God, yet it is a simple matter of fact that the difficulties are so great that unaided reason falls into many and grievous errors in its search for God. The knowledge of faith is free from these errors. Furthermore, even the most highly developed human reason, working under the most favorable natural circumstances, is held within decided limits in its quest for the truths about God. It cannot penetrate the veil of mystery; it cannot even suspect the reality of the inner life of God or know of the divine scheme which actually prevails in the universe and which is expressed in the mysteries of the supernatural life, of the Incarnation, and of the Redemption. These truths are known only through revelation, and they become our own personal knowledge only when we accept God's revelation by making an act of faith.

Faith, then, is the first step in the appreciation and intelligent observance of our duties towards God. By faith we know what God really is and what we are. It is scarcely necessary to enumerate in this chapter the sublime truths of faith. They are contained substantially in the Apostles' Creed and unfolded in word and gesture and song in the liturgical ceremonies by which the Church teaches her children. But it should be mentioned here that any growth in faith, any progress in the knowledge of God and His perfections which comes through reading or study or prayer is not only a fine practice of the commandments but is also a most excellent preparation for living in the spirit of the commandments. And as for teaching, we teach the commandments best when we ourselves

[241]

know God intimately and when we impart this knowledge to our pupils before telling them that they must do this, must not do that, and so forth.

Through faith we are made aware of a vast number of relationships that exist between ourselves and God. He is our Creator, our Helper, our sovereign Lord, our Redeemer, our best Friend, our Father, our Goal. Yet, if we carefully examine these relationships, we shall find that, roughly speaking, they can be grouped under two heads: some emphasize our union with and similarity to God, others emphasize the distinction and distance between ourselves and God.

Suppose we consider first the relationships of distance and distinction. These present a grand picture of God as the Being of supreme excellence and absolute dominion, and of ourselves as creatures who depend utterly upon Him. This is a true picture; it is decidedly appropriate that we recognize it and lead our lives according to it. Down to the very core of our being we are creatures, and any act of ours which expresses this relationship to God is in perfect harmony with our nature.

Creaturely Acts

Among these creaturely acts, the simplest and most fundamental is that of adoration. The essential characteristic of adoration is perfect homage, the homage due to God alone. It is the acknowledgement of God's supreme excellence and our absolute dependence on Him. It may be expressed internally by a simple act of the will; it may be externalized by various gestures, such as the genuflection; or it may seek outlet in the other forms of worship known as the prayer of praise, the prayer of petition, the taking of vows and oaths. Basically, these various acts are but modifications of the one fundamental act of worship. The prayer of praise is adoration with emphasis on the acknowledgement of God's excellence; the prayer of petition is adoration with insistence on our dependence; a vow is adoration expressed by partial or total consecration of oneself to God; an oath is adoration in that it pays tribute to one aspect of divine excellence, God's infinite truthfulness.

Besides being personal and individual, the worship of God must be social as well, for we depend on God not merely as individuals but also as a community. Social worship demands a fixed time for its exercise and definite forms for its manifestation. Hence the propriety of days set aside as God's days, days on which acts of religion and rest from merely secular occupations play the principal part. Hence too the need of that chief of all social acts of worship—sacrifice, a common act of adoration by which the whole community, through its legitimate ministers, makes an offering to God as an acknowledgement of His supreme dominion over the community and of the complete dependence of the community on God.

Social worship, from the very fact that it is external and common, must be regulated; and what norm is more appropriate than that which Almighty God Himself has established in giving us the Holy Sacrifice of the Mass and in founding the Church with power to regulate this act of worship and to establish minor forms?

Adoration in all its forms is reserved to God alone. But it is natural enough that in the sphere of religion we should find a condition similar to that which exists in practically all secular governments and which, if history tells us rightly, is well-nigh as old as government itself. Earthly rulers have their ministers, and it is an accepted custom among men to pay honor to these ministers according to their dignity. In much the same way, God has communicated His excellence to creatures in varying degrees—a fact which forms the basis for the special acts of veneration that we pay to Mary and the saints. This seems so much in accord with human practice in other matters that one wonders why people at times strongly object to it. We honor Mary and the saints because they reflect the divine excellence in a special way; we direct petitions to them because we know that God, whose special friends they are, wishes to honor them by granting His favors through their intercession.

We have mentioned God and His saints. Now let us say a brief word about reverence for the things of God. As we pay Him supreme worship, it is surely appropriate to show a special reverence to everything connected with that worship: the house of God, the sacred vessels, the persons consecrated to Him, the word of God, and of course the holy name of God. All these things represent God, and in honoring them we honor Him.

The acts of virtue thus far enumerated are more fully explained in any theological treatise on the virtue of religion. Like the virtue of justice among human beings, they all emphasize the distinction between ourselves and God. As such, they are distinctively creaturely acts.

Love and Hope

Yet, though we are distinct from God, we are not wholly different from Him; though an infinite distance separates us from Him, in a true sense we are one with Him. Even reason tells us of a similarity to God that is ours in the possession of intellect and free will, and of a special yearning for God which is a property of our spiritual and immortal souls. But faith, in giving us a knowledge of the supernatural order, tells us of a similarity to God and of an ultimate assimilation to God which reason could not so much as suspect. We are children of God, sharers in His own divine nature, members of the divine family, with the destiny of sharing His own happiness in the beatific vision. The distance of creatureship is bridged by the intimacy of friendship; and, though submissive worship is never to be neglected, yet in the present order it yields the primacy to filial love in our dealings with God.

Since God has chosen to deal with us on terms of loving friendship, it is most appropriate that we live according to this relationship. To do so is to live a life of charity, which expresses itself in various ways. It rejoices in the perfections of God; it labors for the fulfillment of God's designs; it accepts God's gift of

Himself and gives itself to God in return. It flees from sin and aims for closer union with God and for perfect conformity to the will of God. Especially does it contemplate God-made-man and strive, as all true love does, for perfect imitation of Him and for the growth of His kingdom in the hearts of men. Though our union with God has already begun, it is still imperfect and breakable. To preserve it and increase it unto the perfection of heaven is difficult; without the help of God, it is impossible. But God in His fatherly goodness has promised not only this help but a reward as well for our cooperation. Since we know His goodness, His power and His unwavering fidelity to His promises, it is fitting that we trust Him, that always in perfect confidence we stretch out our hands to Him as a child reaches out for his parents. Such is the worship of hope.

Devotion

All the acts thus far enumerated are in perfect accord with the commandments that contain our duties to God. To perform such acts, to cultivate such virtues, is to live in the spirit of these commandments. This is not a dry, mechanical process; these acts do not issue from a sterile soul. They presuppose in the soul a certain disposition that theologians call "devotion."

Perhaps it is well for us, particularly if we be educators, to realize that many people have a false idea of religious devotion. They look upon it as something sentimental, something highly emotional, something they might want to experience only when their friends are not present. That is a silly notion. In all other affairs devotion has a lofty signification. Men speak with respect and awe of a soldier devoted to his country, of a husband devoted to his wife, of parents devoted to their children, of a doctor devoted to his duty, and so forth. In all these uses, devotion means something solid—a spirit of self-sacrifice and of true heroism. Yet in the religious sphere the word has a "fluffy" connotation; the mere accidentals are frequently mistaken for the substance.

As a matter of plain fact, religious devotion is the highest of all forms of devotion. It is a ready will to worship God, to serve and love Him as He deserves. It is the most appropriate and the noblest form of hero-worship. It is God-worship—the perfect willingness to acknowledge God for what He is and ourselves for what we are. It is the first fruit of a lively faith, and the very soul of all the other acts of virtue enumerated here.

A life lived according to the pattern sketched in this article is a beautiful life. The greater the number of men who lead such lives, the more does moral beauty shine resplendent in the universe. To labor for this in ourselves and others is our apostolate.

The Church and Moral Beauty

One concluding word: nothing so strikingly illustrates the true beauty of worship as the living Church herself. It sometimes impresses and consoles our people when we show them that through membership in the Church they help to conserve this beauty in the world and are thus contributors to a spiritual achievement of almost unbelievable grandeur. Throughout the world they have built magnificent churches where the one true Sacrifice, as well as other forms of worship, is offered. This worship is conducted with exquisite pageantry and with the finest of this world's goods. Daily and hourly in the name of the Church, there ascends to God the most reverent of all prayers, the Divine Office. Our Catholic people have a wealth of religious festivals in honor of God and His Mysteries; they venerate Mary, the Mother of God, and the angels and saints, His special friends; they cherish the written word of God and reverence the living teaching authority that He established. They have doctrines and a moral code of transcendent beauty. They have a priesthood dedicated wholly to priestly work. Thousands of their men and women are consecrated to God by vow. In toil and sacrifice, they have built countless schools to safeguard the religious education of youth; and there is no work of mercy excluded from the stupendous program of charity that the Church is ever conducting.

All those things blend together to form the sweet incense of worship that is constantly being offered to God through the Holy Catholic Church. It is a living expression of the first table of the Decalogue and of the great commandment of love.

chapter 13

How Often Must We Pray?

DURING the years I have been teaching religious, particularly sisters, I have often been confronted with this problem: "Examinations of conscience sometimes contain the question 'Did I miss my morning and evening prayers, and my grace before and after meals?' Does this question mean that such daily prayers are obligatory? And if they are not obligatory, how are we to explain the question to children?"

The problem, be it noted, concerns obligation. It pertains therefore to moral, not to ascetical, theology; and it is as a moral problem that I intend to treat it. But before I touch upon the actual question, I should like to make some preliminary observations that may prevent misunderstandings.

Preliminary Observations

I lay claim to no special knowledge, acquired or infused, natural or supernatural, concerning the teaching of catechism to children. In fact, I may state quite frankly that at the end of the one year of my Jesuit life in which I had the duty of teaching catechism to third-graders I was thoroughly convinced that I had not reached their minds with a single idea.

[249]

As a fellow Jesuit once put it to me when we were returning home after a catechism session, "Every time
I leave that class, it's with a feeling of having been
thwarted."

Despite that year of frustration, I still retain certain notions concerning what ought and what ought
not to be taught to children. For one thing, I believe
it is much better to show children (and perhaps
adults, too) the fittingness, the loveliness, and the
beauty of the various acts of prayer than to try to
make precise distinctions concerning their obligation
to pray.[1] If they love prayer, they will pray; and thus
they will fulfill these obligations even though they
cannot define them. This seems to be in keeping with
the common opinion of theologians to the effect that
Catholics who lead a devout life need never worry
about failing to fulfill their various duties to pray.

Nevertheless, it is not right, merely in order to
encourage children to do good, to foster an erroneous notion concerning their obligations. Consequently, when any book or statement gives them the
impression that they have a strict obligation though
in reality they do not, that impression should be tactfully corrected.

As regards daily prayers in particular, I might observe before discussing the main question that, even
if there should be an obligation to pray every day,
there is certainly no duty to pray at definite times of
the day, for example, in the morning or evening.
Evidently these are fitting times, yet pious Catholics
who humbly confess that they did not say their morn-

1 See the preceding chapter.

[250]

ing prayers but said them later in the day surely have a false conscience if they think that in so acting they sin.

Moreover, even if there should be an obligation to pray daily, there is clearly no obligation to say the prayers in some definite position. Some people seem to think that if they do not kneel when they pray they are doing wrong. A notion of this kind should be corrected—or, better still, prevented.

Now for the question: Is it obligatory, at least under pain of venial sin, to pray every day? Official pronouncements of the Church do not answer this question. A casual reading of Sacred Scripture seems to answer it in the affirmative. For instance, we are told: "Pray without ceasing" (I Thessalonians 5:17); "We ought always to pray" (Luke 18:1); and "Be instant in prayer" (Colossians 4:2). Texts like these appear to demand at least daily prayer; yet we know from the traditional teaching of approved theologians that such texts need not be taken in their full literal force. In part, at least, they express a counsel, not a command. To know the extent of the obligation we have to turn to the writings of the moral theologians.

Meaning of Prayer

What do theologians mean by prayer? In general they distinguish between prayer in the strict sense and prayer in the wide sense. In the strict sense prayer refers to petition, and it is defined as the "asking for becoming things from God." In the wide sense it means "any lifting of the soul to God" or any actual "communion with God." In this latter sense prayer includes acts of faith, hope, love, adoration, petition, thanksgiving, praise, contrition, and so forth.

It seems unquestionable that when we consider the problem of daily prayers we are referring not merely to the prayer of petition but to prayer in the wide sense. To determine the exact obligation of praying, therefore, we ought to study what theologians have to say about the necessity of each of the acts mentioned in the previous paragraph. As a matter of fact, with reference to the necessity of prayer, moralists do not treat all these acts but only the principal ones: faith, hope, charity, contrition, and petition. These five acts, as treated by theologians, are primarily considered as internal acts; though at times, of course, as when we speak of the necessity of certain acts in connection with confession, some external expression is understood. Besides these various internal acts, theologians also treat of the necessity of social worship, which might include in some way many of the prayers not specifically mentioned elsewhere. A brief survey of these various sections of moral theology will give us all the background we need for a correct answer to the question: Are daily prayers of obligation?

Various Acts

The Catholic life is a supernatural life; and faith is the foundation of supernatural living. It is evident, therefore, that faith must play an important part in the Catholic life; in fact, a truly devout life undoubtedly includes many acts of faith, at least implicitly, every day. But the fervent life is not the measure of obligation, since obligation refers to the minimum.

When they speak of the obligation of making acts of faith, theologians are very conservative in estimating the required frequency.

Treating of the necessity of making acts of faith, moralists first consider the nature of faith itself and its importance in the Christian life. From this consideration they conclude that every Catholic must make an act of faith at the beginning of his conscious moral life when he first realizes that God has revealed certain truths to be believed. Another occasion that calls for an act of faith is when the Church solemnly defines a certain doctrine and thus imposes upon us the duty of accepting it as divinely revealed. Besides specifying these two occasions, the most that theologians can say about the precept of faith in itself is that we must make acts of faith "at times" during life. Some have tried to define this obligation more accurately in terms of years, months, or weeks. These opinions are certainly worth reading; but they are merely opinions, not binding on anyone.

In the preceding paragraph I have indicated duties imposed on all Catholics by the precept of faith itself. Besides these, there are certain occasions when some other precept or special circumstance includes at least implicitly the necessity of making an act of faith. For instance, the duties of making acts of hope, charity, and contrition include the duty of making implicit acts of faith because such acts are impossible without faith. So does the duty of making a good confession or a good Communion. In all these cases, however, faith is not necessarily a separate act. Also, if one is facing a strong temptation which he cannot

[253]

overcome without an act of faith, this act is obligatory. And if one has denied his faith by the sin of heresy or by apostasy from the true religion, he must, in reparation, make a new act of acceptance of the revealed truths he has denied.

The theology on the necessity of acts of hope follows much the same pattern as I have outlined with regard to faith. From the dogmatic and ascetical points of view it would be difficult to exaggerate the importance of hope. It must be present in the repentance of the sinner, in the heroism of the saint, and in the salutary perseverance of all the just. But concerning its prescribed frequency one must be cautious. Like faith, an act of hope is required at the beginning of one's moral life and "at times" during life. And like faith, it is at least implicitly required in certain other acts—for example, in an act of contrition, in a good confession, and in any effective prayer for grace. Also, an act of hope is required in reparation for a sin of desperation.

We next consider the best of all prayers, the act of love of God. That there are certain special occasions when an act of charity is imperative, is evident. For example, if a man is dying in the state of mortal sin and cannot receive a sacrament, he can save his soul only by making an act of perfect contrition, which includes an act of charity. Again, if a person is in the state of mortal sin and must receive one of the sacraments of the living but cannot go to confession, he is bound to regain the state of grace by means of perfect contrition.

Even apart from these special occasions, one must

at least occasionally during life make explicit acts of
charity. This is the constant and universal teaching
of eminent theologians, and the only teaching that
the Church will tolerate. Absurd opinions such as
"It is enough to make an act of charity once in a life
time, or once every five years" have been condemned.
How anyone could hold opinions of this nature in
view of the facts that the very essence of the New
Law is charity and that Sacred Scripture urges us
again and again to love God is somewhat of a mystery.

Yet it is one thing to say that we must make acts
of charity occasionally or even frequently and quite
another to say how often. There is nothing defined
on this point, and the theologians cannot determine
it. All that can be said with certainty is that acts of
charity should be made occasionally, or perhaps
rather often, during life.

In the preceding paragraphs I have referred to the
act of contrition. My remarks were merely passing
references. A summary of the approved teaching concerning the necessity of this particular act would run
somewhat as follows. It is a conditional obligation
and depends on the fact that one has sinned. The
Blessed Virgin, for instance, could not make an act
of contrition—and therefore could have no obligation
to do so—because she never sinned. But for one who
has sinned, contrition of some kind is an absolute
requirement for forgiveness. For one who has committed a mortal sin, this clearly means that he has a
serious obligation to make an act of contrition (perfect or imperfect, according to circumstances) on the
following occasions: when he is in danger of death,

when he makes his yearly confession, when he is obliged for some special reason to acquire the state of grace (for example, when he receives a sacrament of the living). Venial sin does not require confession and is not an obstacle to the fruitful reception of the sacraments of the living; hence it seems that there is no definite occasion when contrition for venial sin is absolutely called for. Confession, of course, would make it conditionally necessary: that is, if one who has only venial sins wishes to go to confession, he is obliged to make an act of contrition.

We come now to prayer in its strictest theological meaning—petition. This kind of prayer may be considered under a twofold aspect: it is an act of worship of God, and it is a means of helping ourselves. As an act of worship, petition expresses our reverence for and dependence on God. Understood in this sense, prayer is certainly of obligation for all men, independently of their personal sanctity and of their special personal needs. Yet, if we limit our consideration of prayer to this sense, we can say no more about the frequency of the obligation than we said about the necessity of making acts of faith, hope, and charity. We can simply say that every man, even the least tempted, even the most perfect, even one confirmed in grace, must pray occasionally. His very nature demands that he express his dependence on God in this way; but neither reason nor revelation tells clearly just how often he must so express himself.

Prayer, however, is not merely a means of honoring God; it is also a personal necessity. In the providence of God, humble petition is the ordinary means of obtaining His blessings, particularly His grace,

and grace is a necessity for both salvation and sanctification. Since man is obliged to do at least what is
required for his salvation, he is certainly obliged to
pray.

But how often must we direct our petition to God?
Must it be every day, or every time we need help?
Theologians, having carefully considered the data
afforded by Scripture and tradition, do not feel justified in giving an unqualified "yes" to such questions.
The most that they can give as a *general* rule is that
we must pray "very often." Beyond this, the answer
is relative; some need to pray more frequently than
others.

As regards the prayers we have considered in the
preceding paragraphs, one difficulty in estimating the
obligations is that this must be done almost entirely
without the help of definite statements by the
Church. The case is different with regard to social
worship; hence we need but mention this topic very
briefly. The Mass is our principal form of social worship, and the Church has stated quite definitely that
we must assist at Mass on all Sundays and on clearly
determined feasts of obligation.

Conclusions

I suppose that up to this point my discussion sounds
more mathematical than religious. If it does, that is
unintentional; I have not been inspired by any love
of mathematics. I have no desire to urge people to
count their prayers or measure their obligations. And
I earnestly recommend, for the comfort of all, the
common opinion of theologians to which I referred
earlier in this chapter: namely, that those who lead

a good Catholic life need not be concerned about any possible failure to fulfill their various duties to pray.

Nevertheless, mathematics has its uses; and one use is right here, in this conclusion. We have to ask ourselves whether all the duties to pray that have been outlined in this article add up to an obligation to say daily prayers. The answer is negative. If we prescind for a moment from the relative duty of praying for the graces we need, it seems that all the other duties can generally be fulfilled by the devout attendance at Mass at the prescribed times. The necessity of prayer for personal needs may increase this somewhat, but there is no evidence that it is a daily duty for everyone.

Do all moral theologians agree with the conclusion that daily prayer is not of strict obligation? The answer seems to be "yes and no." They agree with the conclusion *in theory*, but many prefer to give a qualified answer *for practice*. They would say: "Theoretically, there is no obligation to pray every day. But in practice there is usually a sin in the omission of these prayers, because when daily prayers are omitted without a sufficient reason this is often due to a small fault of laziness, sensuality, or human respect."

This formula, or a somewhat similar one, is sponsored by eminent theologians; and catechists who wish to follow it in explaining the duty of praying are certainly justified in doing so. But I would not recommend it. I find it confusing. It says, on the one hand, that daily prayers are not of obligation; yet, on the other, it demands a sufficient reason under pain of sin for omitting them. This seems to beg the entire question; for if there is no obligation to say daily prayers, why should a reason be required *under pain of sin* for omitting them? As for the statement that failure to say these prayers could be a sin of laziness, it seems to ignore completely the distinction between imperfection and venial sin.[2] Laziness is not a sin in the strict sense; it is an inordinate disposition or tendency, and it becomes sinful only when it leads to the neglect of some duty binding under pain of sin. In other words, laziness is an imperfection when it induces one to act against a counsel (for instance, to break a rule which does not bind under pain of sin), and it is a sin when it leads one to violate a precept (for instance, to miss Sunday Mass in whole or in part).[3] And what I have said of laziness is similarly true of such things as sensuality and human respect.

Because of these difficulties, I would not personally recommend the formula. I prefer the practical explanation given by Father Tanquerey in his moral theology, which may be roughly translated as follows:

> The faithful are to be urged to pray daily, especially in the morning to ask the graces they need for the day, and in the evening to thank God for benefits received, to make an act of contrition for their sins, and to commend their souls to God before going to sleep. Those

[2] Some authors hold that a positive imperfection is a venial sin. These men might logically defend the formula I am here criticizing. But many moralists who propose this kind of formula also hold firmly to the distinction between positive imperfections and venial sins.

[3] Even here, when we speak of the "sin of laziness," it is not a specific kind of sin, but merely the source of sin. This is obvious from the fact that when one misses Mass through laziness, all that he is obliged to confess is the fact that he missed Mass.

who omit their morning and evening prayers do not sin directly by this omission; but experience proves that, all other things being equal, those who do not say these prayers fall into sin more frequently than those who say them.[4]

One final point. In view of all that has been said, what is a catechism teacher to do when the examination of conscience for children includes the question: "Did I miss my morning and evening prayers, and my grace before and after meals?" Before I answer, let me recall my own experience in teaching third-graders. With this experience in mind, I have not the temerity to suggest the precise method of illuminating young minds. All that I dare suggest is that the teacher try in some way to convey the following ideas to the children:

"This question does not mean that you would commit a sin every time you omit these prayers. The question is put there to remind you that all of us must often pray and that morning and evening are especially fitting times for prayer. If you do not pray at these times, there is a good chance that you won't pray at other times, either; and this would mean that you do not pray even when you really need it, and that would be a sin. So, keep the habit of saying these daily prayers, and when you go to confession check up on yourselves to see whether you have been saying them. If you find that you often miss your daily prayers, you will know that you are getting a bad habit, and you ought to correct it."

[4] A. Tanquerey, *Synopsis Theologiae Moralis et Pastoralis*, II (1936), n. 861.

chapter 14

Subjective Sin

THE points to be treated in this brief chapter on sin will probably be more concrete and intelligible if they are centered about a problem that I once gave a group of sisters during a summer session. The problem runs as follows:

Florina, a very devout woman, examines her conscience before confession and decides to accuse herself in this way: "I ate some meat on Friday because I forgot it was Friday. I told a lie; but I thought it was all right because, if I hadn't lied, my brother might have had to go to jail. I belong to a confraternity that obliges its members say the rosary every day, but I deliberately omitted my rosary for several days. I missed Mass one Sunday because our car broke down right outside the house; as we live way out in the country, there was no way of getting to Mass." Which, if any, of these accusations might be sufficient matter for absolution?

In its most obvious sense, this problem deals with the sacrament of penance, for Florina cannot receive absolution unless she includes in her confession what is called "sufficient matter" for absolution. Basically, however, the problem is concerned with a fundamental distinction between formal and merely material sin—a distinction explained by theologians in their treatises on actual sin. I say that the problem is basically concerned with this distinction because only formal sin can be matter for absolution; hence the student's main task is to determine whether Florina's accusations contain any manifestation of formal sin.

Actual sin may be defined as any act or omission contrary to the eternal law of God. The eternal law of God includes not only the commands and prohibitions that come directly from God (as in the case with the natural law and the precepts given through divine revelation), but also the valid commands and prohibitions laid on us by legitimate human authority. "Act," as used in the definition, may refer to an external deed (such as theft), a word (as in detraction), or merely a thought (such as a denial of faith). And a sinful omission, of course, will refer to just the contrary of these: namely, a failure to do a prescribed deed (for example, to go to Mass on Sunday), to say a word (for example, to profess one's faith externally when that is obligatory), or to make a prescribed internal act (for example, an act of perfect contrition when it is necessary for the salvation of one's soul).

When theologians speak of formal sin they are referring to and emphasizing the subjective elements of sin. Formal sin is had only when a person is conscious of an obligation to do or to omit something and when he freely acts against this obligation by neglecting to do what is commanded or by doing what is forbidden. There must be some consciousness of obligation and some freedom; otherwise there can be no formal sin. Only formal sin is sin in the real and full sense of the word. Only formal sin makes a person subjectively guilty in the sight of God; and therefore only formal sin can be the subject matter for contrition and sacramental absolution.

To refer to an act or an omission as a material sin is to emphasize the objective character of the act or omission. In other words, it simply states that such and such an act or omission is against the law. The catechism teacher who explains the various violations of divine and human laws is using the word "sin" in the material sense. He says, "It is a sin to steal, to murder, to lie, to miss Mass on Sunday unless one is excused or dispensed." This does not necessarily mean that everyone who steals, murders, or lies is subjectively guilty of sin. If a man who has absolutely no claim to my money takes a roll of bills from my desk (for the sake of the example we can suppose that I have a roll of bills in my desk), his act is materially, or objectively, a theft. But if he thinks the money is his, or if he is a kleptomaniac who has no control over himself in such matters, he is not subjectively guilty of theft. He could not make an act of contrition for that theft, and he could not receive absolution from that sin, for it is not a formal sin. The soldier who puts a bullet through the head of his fatally wounded captain performs an act which must be materially, or objectively, catalogued as murder; but if the soldier really thinks that he ought to do this, he is not formally guilty of murder. If that were all that he had done since his last confession he could not receive absolution unless he included sins of his past life.

When people ask our advice concerning the future, we give our counsel according to objective standards. We say, "You must go to Mass Sunday because you do not have a good reason for staying away"; "You may not tell a lie"; "It would be a sin to do that"; and so forth. But when people come to confession, the priest has to attend to the subjective side. Usually this is not difficult, since people generally know when they are doing wrong and they are not generally acting under any compulsion that deprives them of freedom. However, there are exceptions; and these exceptions, especially with regard to correct knowledge, are by no means so infrequent as to be negligible.

These preliminary observations about the distinction between formal and material sin contain the essential notions that should be recalled before solving the problems pertaining to Florina's contemplated confession.

Florina ate meat on Friday because she forgot it was Friday. Even the inattentive young boy by the window can advise Florina correctly on that. If she forgot it was Friday, he would say, she must have thought it was all right to eat the meat; and if she thought it was all right to eat the meat, then she committed no subjective sin. Her act was objectively against the law, but it involved no subjective guilt. Florina may confess it if that makes her feel better, but the confessor cannot absolve from it.

[264]

She told a lie, but when she told the lie she thought it was all right. This accusation involves several possibilities. One of the obvious possibilities is that Florina did not really lie but rather used a legitimate mental reservation. Unlearned people seldom know the technical distinction between mental reservation and lying, yet they often "have a feeling" that there ought to be some distinction. However, since they do not know the technical language, they are apt to express themselves in the same way that Florina has chosen to accuse herself in confession.

Even if Florina did tell a dyed-in-the-wool lie, she did not sin formally in so doing, for apparently she was not conscious of any obligation not to tell that particular lie. In all good faith she simply acted according to the false doctrine that the end justifies the means. Florina may need instruction on that point, but she does not need and cannot get absolution.

Several of the sisters to whom I assigned this problem were not easily convinced that Florina's ignorance would excuse her from the guilt of lying, and against the "easy" solution they advanced some objections that might be profitably considered here. For instance, one objection goes somewhat like this: "In all our catechism classes, even with small children, we teach that it is always wrong to lie. If Florina is any kind of a Catholic at all—and the case says she is a 'devout woman'—she ought to know this. She *should have known* better." This is an interesting objection because it expresses an error which is all too common among conscientious people. One good Catholic will forget it is Friday and eat meat, as

Florina did, and then will upbraid himself afterwards because he *should have* realized it was Friday. Another will make what he thinks is a perfectly inoffensive remark and then, after he has discovered that the remark wounded another's feelings, will chide himself because he *should have* foreseen this. And so on.

It is well to remember that conscience is an actual judgment; it expresses what we do think, do realize, at the time we act. And God judges us on what we do think, do realize—not on what we should have thought or should have realized. We can regret actions that were performed through ignorance or through a lack of realization of possible consequences, and we can learn from them to be more careful in the future, but we cannot make formal sin out of such acts.

"But, isn't there such a thing as culpable ignorance? And could not Florina's lie be sinful by reason of culpable ignorance?" I can answer these questions more easily than I can explain my answers. The answers are "Yes" and "No." Yes, there is such a thing as culpable ignorance; and no, Florina's lie would not be sinful by reason of such ignorance.

The full explanation of culpable ignorance is—if I may use the word—tricky. Suppose we simply illustrate it by an example. A young man is studying medicine and at this particular period in his course the professor is explaining the use of a very dangerous drug. The young man neglects his studies at this time, even though he realizes this is something he ought to know and even though he foresees that the wrong use of this drug may do much harm. In deliberately neglecting his studies, with the consciousness of an obligation to learn this important matter now, the young man would be sinning formally.

Suppose that this young man, still ignorant of some very serious dangers of this drug, goes out to practice medicine. Because of his ignorance he gives the drug to one of his patients and great harm results. If the young man is still ignorant of the danger of the drug at the time he prescribes it—and we are supposing that this is the case—he does not sin *when he gives the prescription*. His sin was committed at the time he consciously neglected his obligation to learn about the drug; and that is the only time he sinned formally. He can, of course, justly be obliged to make good the damages to his patient, because these damages are the result of wilful neglect on his part to acquire knowledge which members of his profession should have.

As for Florina, it is hardly likely that her lie is the result of culpable ignorance. As a child she may have neglected her catechism a bit, as many children do; but, even if her ignorance were culpable, this would simply mean that once upon a time she was guilty of some sin (a tiny one, if I may say so) by neglecting to study her catechism.

In these few paragraphs I have merely scratched the surface of the subject of culpable ignorance. But that scratch is enough for our present purpose. It shows us that the first half of Florina's confession is worthless from the point of view of absolution. So far, the most the confessor could do for her would be to give her some advice and, of course, a blessing.

The third of Florina's self-accusations is interesting in that it shows us what might be called the other side of the picture. We have seen that in her first two accusations there may have been material sin, but there was no formal sin; in this third point there may be formal sin without any real material sin. Let us examine the case briefly.

Florina deliberately missed the rosary prescribed by her confraternity. If I were a betting man and had something to bet, I would readily wager a fat sum that the confraternity does not prescribe this rosary under pain of sin. In other words, I doubt very much whether Florina really had a strict obligation to say the rosary; hence the omission of the rosary would not be objectively sinful. Yet, if Florina thought it was a sin to omit the rosary, and then, conscious of this self-created obligation, she deliberately omitted it, she did sin formally. It is possible that this was her frame of mind; and if it was, then she has here some matter, though slight, for absolution. A confessor would have to investigate a bit before coming to a conclusion and giving absolution.

A false conscience, as we no doubt know and as we have just seen in Florina's accusations, can work two ways: it can free one from an obligation and it can impose on one an obligation that would not otherwise exist. In a certain sense, therefore, it is true that "if you think you sin, you do sin." But only in a limited sense. And it was to show this limitation that I introduced Florina's fourth accusation into the problem.

Florina missed Mass because she simply could not go. In this case there was no real material sin because the law does not oblige in such circumstances. Furthermore, even if Florina thought she was sinning by missing Mass, there would still be no formal sin, no subjective guilt, because she was not free to go to Mass. Even a false conscience cannot make an act a formal sin if the act is not deliberate.

One of the examples theologians ordinarily use to illustrate the fact that freedom is necessary for subjective guilt is the case of a man who is in prison on Sunday and who cannot get to Mass. If this man is a truly simple soul—and for the sake of the example the theologians suppose him to be a truly simple soul —he may think that he sins by missing Mass. But though he thought so all through the day and far into the night, the fact remains the same: he simply does not sin, because he is not physically free. And our friend Florina, though not in prison, is equivalently deprived of her freedom when her car breaks down.

Physical circumstances are not the only factors that deprive one of the power of sinning formally by removing freedom. Sometimes people find themselves in a sort of mental jam that has the same effect. I can illustrate this statement by returning to Florina's second accusation—her lie to save her brother. As it happened, she thought it was all right to tell the lie, and we have already solved the case on that supposition. But it will do no harm to make another supposition. We might suppose, for instance, that at the time of telling the lie Florina sincerely thought that it would be a sin to lie and also thought that it would be a sin to let her brother go to jail. In other words, her mental state was this: "If I lie, I sin; and if I do not lie, I sin."

A weird state of mind indeed! Nevertheless, it is not so uncommon as to be merely theoretical. Theologians refer to it as the case of the perplexed conscience, and they give three simple rules for dealing with it when it occurs. The first rule is to obtain advice if possible. Secondly, if advice is not obtainable, the person should try to do what appears to be the less evil. Thirdly, if one cannot determine which is the lesser evil, one may choose either side of the dilemma, and there will be no formal sin. Florina, therefore, would not sin formally whether she lied or did not lie; for in thinking that both alternatives were sinful, she really deprived herself of the power to sin, because formal sin presupposes freedom to avoid sin.

Extremely scrupulous people often experience a mental confusion somewhat similar to what I have just described as the "perplexed conscience." Because of their oppressive fear of sin they see it everywhere, whether they act or whether they refrain from acting. Of course, they cannot sin formally while in such a state of mind.

These notes on Florina's case have all been directed towards the distinction between formal and material sin. An act may be materially sinful, but not formally so; and vice versa. The explanation might be carried a step further by showing how an act might be a mortal sin materially, and only a venial sin formally; or a venial sin materially and mortal sin formally. But this distinction between mortal and venial sin is another story. It will have to wait for some other occasion. For the present it is sufficient to have pointed out that only Florina's third accusation could contain any subjective sin and be matter for absolution.

chapter 15

The Law of
Integral Confession

ACCORDING to the traditional teaching of the Church, our Lord Himself, in instituting the sacrament of penance under the form of a judicial procedure, implicitly commanded the confession of all mortal sins committed after baptism. The priest, as judge, must know the "whole cause," at least substantially; and each mortal sin pertains to the substance of this judgment, because any single mortal sin is enough to keep the sinner separated from God and deserving of eternal damnation.

This traditional teaching was solemnly confirmed by the Council of Trent. Especially since the time of Trent theologians have been very careful to explain what is now known as the "divine law of integral confession," and it is hard to conceive of a catechism which does not make some mention of this important law. The Baltimore Catechism refers to it when it speaks of our obligation to make an "entire confession."

Theological explanations go much beyond the words of a catechism. In regard to the law of integ-

[273]

rity, it seems worth while to give here some of the principal points contained in the ordinary theological explanations. This for two reasons: first, it is good "background" for catechists; and secondly, it sometimes contributes much to personal peace of mind to have a rather precise knowledge of the extent of this law. The following comments on the law are offered with the hope that they will be of some help along one or both of these lines.

Stating the law first in rather general terms, we may say that everyone who receives the sacrament of penance is obliged to confess *his mortal sins in such a way that the confessor can judge the kinds of sins committed and the number of times each sin was committed.* A few comments on some of the italicized words may prove helpful.

Mortal Sins

It goes without saying that this law does not refer to sins committed before baptism. Such sins are completely remitted by baptism, and they are never matter for confession. Evidently, too, the law does not include sins already confessed and absolved. The obligation of confessing these has already been fulfilled; they are no longer *necessary* matter but, like venial sins, they are *optional* matter. It helps to include such forgiven sins in subsequent confessions, because this is an added incentive to contrition and to a continued purpose of amendment, and also because, by the subsequent confessions, it is possible to reduce more and more the temporal punishment that might still be due for these sins. God has given us no assurance that He remits *all* the punishment due to sin by the mere fact that He forgives the sin.

The expression "mortal sin" must be taken at its face value. This means, if I may use the term, a full-fledged mortal sin: that is, one that the penitent himself considered mortal at the time he did it, and which he committed with "sufficient reflection and full consent of the will." It may happen at times that a person does something that he thinks to be only a venial sin, or perhaps no sin at all, then later on learns that such an act is a mortal sin. Such a person need not be disquieted. It was not a mortal sin *for him*; therefore he neither had nor has an obligation to confess it. Past acts are not to be judged by present knowledge.

Kinds of Sin

Moral theologians make many refined distinctions in classifying sins. Though ordinary people would not be expected to know these refinements, they should know the principal ways in which sins differ from one another, and they are bound to confess their sins according to this knowledge: that is, they must confess in such a way that the confessor knows the distinct kinds of mortal sins they thought they committed. In general they should avoid two extremes. One extreme is a detailed description of what they did; the other is a very general statement that forces a confessor to ask embarrassing questions which could easily be avoided.

Putting aside all technicalities, we can say that the penitent is expected to give the confessor in his own language a simple answer to the following four questions.

1) *Was the sin internal or external?* In other words, was it merely a sin of thought, or was it externalized by word or action? For example, it is not sufficient to say "I intended to steal" if one actually did steal.

2) *What commandment or virtue was violated?* These are the two ordinary ways of classifying sins. Either method is permissible in confessing: for example, one may say, "I sinned against the 7th Commandment" or "I sinned against justice." If the next question is correctly answered, it will include the answer to this present one.

3) *How was the commandment or virtue violated?* A confession in which one stated merely the commandment or virtue violated would be too general and would force the confessor to ask questions in order to determine more precisely the kind of sin committed. The commandments and virtues can be violated in various ways, and it is in distinguishing these varieties of sin that theologians make their finest distinctions. These refinements, as was stated, are not always known; but, generally speaking, the more common distinctions (for example, those listed in the catechism) are known and should be manifested to the confessor. For instance, a man guilty of serious calumny is not sufficiently definite in his confession if he merely states, "I sinned seriously against justice" or "I sinned seriously against the eighth commandment." He must specify that he spoke falsely against his neighbor in a serious matter.

4) *Were there any special circumstances that would*

seriously alter the nature of the sin committed? Practically speaking, this question refers to those circumstances in which a person has more than one serious obligation for doing or avoiding something. Therefore, when he sins he violates two distinct obligations. For instance, the same act may be a serious sin against justice and against the vow of poverty, or against the virtue and the vow of chastity. Scandal given by a superior who is charged with the spiritual care of his subjects is different from scandal given by others. Sins against parents (hatred, refusal to help them when in serious need, or insulting them) differ from the same sins committed against others, because the special relationship often adds a special obligation.

(Note: The distinctions mentioned in this last point, as well as the entire method of confessing sins according to the four questions, are best taught by examples and by frequent repetition. As a final safeguard for those who might not learn very well, it is advisable to warn all that if they have something they think should be confessed and they do not know just how to say it, they should tell their confessor that, and he will help them with some simple questions.)

Number of Sins

The number of each kind of mortal sin committed must be given as accurately as possible. If the penitent cannot remember the exact number, he is supposed to say "about," and give the number as best he can. If he cannot make even an approximation or calculate the average per day, week, or month, he should tell the confessor that; and it may be that both confessor and penitent will have to leave the matter to God.

Since venial sins are not necessary matter for confession, it is obvious that, if they are confessed, their number need not be given unless the penitent wishes to give it. It seems that children are often taught to confess the exact number of all their sins, even venial sins. Perhaps the teachers look upon this as the simplest practical way of instructing children how to confess. If so, the method has an advantage; but it is well not to insist on it to the extent that children think they have a strict obligation of confessing all their "small sins."

Excuses from Integrity

Our Lord intended the law of integral confession to be a very serious law, yet He did not impose it on us in such a way as to demand the humanly impossible. If we were to phrase the law with perfect accuracy, we should say that we are obliged to confess all our mortal sins (as explained), *insofar as it is possible to do so.* When it is impossible to confess a sin, or a number of sins, the penitent may omit them and still make a good confession, but he is bound to confess them later, if it becomes possible. For a better understanding of the law, it may be well to indicate here some of the standard examples of good, though incomplete, confessions.

Some penitents do not remember a certain mortal sin, even though they examine their consciences diligently. Some remember the sin during the examination of conscience but forget it when they are in the confessional. Since they cannot confess what they do not remember, their confession is good, even though incomplete. The omitted sin (or sins) should be confessed at their next confession if they remember it then. In the meantime they may receive Communion with a good conscience.

Lack of time occasionally excuses one from making a complete confession. We are all familiar now with the case of soldiers before a battle. By making a visible sign of their contrition they signify to the priest that they are sorry for their sins, and he gives them absolution. Their sins are thus manifested only in the most general way. Their action says equivalently: "I am a sinner and I ask pardon for my sins." They receive the sacrament when the priest gives absolution, but they must later make a specific confession, if they can. A similar case might occur in a hospital before an emergency operation.

Sometimes a penitent is excused from the confession of one or many sins because confessing them would expose him to some serious harm. For example, if a sick person were so weak that a prolonged confession would overtax his strength, he would be allowed to make an incomplete confession and confess the remaining sins when he was stronger. Again, circumstances might be such that the penitent could not confess without being overheard by others (for instance, in some hospital wards). Since he is not bound to tell anyone but the confessor his humiliating sins, he could make an incomplete confession and tell the omitted sins when he could enjoy the requisite privacy. Finally, the really scrupulous person affords an example of one who cannot keep the law of material integrity without the danger of serious spiritual harm. It often happens that the attempt to keep the law simply increases the scrupulosity and renders it more incurable. A confessor who judges this to be the case is quite justified in cutting short the confession or even in limiting the scrupulous penitent to a very generic confession. The judgment of individual cases will have to be left to the confessor; but it is important to note that confessors who do limit the confessions of scrupulous penitents are not acting on mere whim, but according to sound theological principles.

In all the foregoing cases, except that of the scrupulous penitent, the omitted sins must be told later. I make exception for the scrupulous penitent for a practical reason: namely, it would be a practical impossibility for him ever to attempt to tell the omitted sins without exposing himself to the danger of a new attack of scruples. Hence, in practice, the only safe course is to consider that the obligation is perpetually suspended.

Shame

Before leaving the subject of incomplete confessions I should like to add a word about the omission of certain humiliating accusations through a sense of fear or shame. The ordinary rule given, I believe, in most, if not all, catechisms, is that we are obliged to confess all our mortal sins, even though we are very much ashamed of them, and that if we do conceal a mortal sin through shame, we make a bad confession and commit a sacrilege.

[280]

This is the ordinary rule, and in teaching it to our pupils we conform to the constant practice of the Church. Nevertheless, it happens at times that some teachers go beyond this rule. In their anxiety to see that the rule is kept, they illustrate it with "horror" stories that manifest a decided lack of sympathy for the weakness of human nature. All of us, whether confessors or teachers or just plain penitents, must remember that there is connected with shame a certain "human" element which may at times weigh considerably with God in favor of the penitent.

A simple analogy will illustrate what I mean. Let us imagine a large number of people who dislike a certain kind of food. Among these people it will be found that the dislike varies in degree. Most of them could probably eat the food if they had to. But very likely there would be a few with appetites so sensitive or prejudices so strong that they could not swallow the food at all.

Shame over humiliating sins follows the same pattern. In general, we are all ashamed of our sins, but we can tell them when we have to. There do seem to be some cases, however, in which shame is so vehement as to be tongue-tying. This is sometimes so with children who have been told frightening stories about the confessional and with adults in regard to certain confessors who have misunderstood or dealt harshly with them or with whom they have to deal on rather intimate terms outside the confessional.

Many theologians recognize the existence of a sense of shame which amounts to an invincible repugnance. It is a subjective difficulty, and a comparatively rare case; and it is not improbable that Almighty God makes allowance for it in enforcing His positive laws. Because the difficulty is subjective and rare, it is dangerous to try to phrase our ordinary rule in such a way as to include it, and perhaps it would not be wise to try to do so. Nevertheless, the realization that these cases do exist should warn us against the telling of certain "horrifying" stories about concealed sins. "And the little boy went to confession. But in the confessional he gave in to his shame and he concealed a mortal sin from the priest. And he left the confessional, his soul black with sacrilege. And then he died, and the devil came for his soul. And he was buried in hell forever." The whole thing is "creepy." It has nothing—except deep contrast—to remind one of the familiar Scripture text: "A bruised reed he will not break . . ." After listening to such stories, many a timid soul has been filled with a dread of confession that lasted for years, even for life.

Concluding Remarks

The foregoing is an explanation of all the essential points pertaining to the law of integral confession. We can conclude with a few remarks about certain practical questions often associated with this obligation.

What about *doubtful* cases? For example, a person may doubt whether he has committed a mortal sin; or he may know that he committed a sin but doubt whether he has confessed it. A good rule, sponsored by many eminent theologians and therefore safe and sound in practice, is the following: if the penitent has a sincere, solid doubt about having committed a mortal sin, or if he has a good reason for believing that he has confessed a sin, he is not obliged to tell it in his present confession. Some are inclined to make exceptions for the lax, but there is no need of making an exception. The real difficulty with lax people is that they are inclined to doubt without solid reasons. In that case they do not really doubt, and the rule does not apply to them. But if, in any individual case, they do really doubt, then they too may follow the general rule.

The *obligation* of confessing a sin, therefore, does not exist in doubtful cases. *Advisability* is another question. Usually it is better to confess it unless one is scrupulous, in which case he should do what his confessor tells him and keep as happy as he can under the circumstances. He will probably be tormented with the thought that the "confessor doesn't understand," but he must learn to take these "misunderstandings" as part of his cross.

Temptations, of course, are not sins; hence they are not matter for absolution in any sense of the word. They may be told in confession—and laudably so—if one wishes advice about them or if one simply wishes to give his confessor a manifestation of conscience. But if told, they should be properly labeled. To say, "I had impure thoughts," when one means that he was merely tempted is hardly a clear way of stating the case.

The mere fact that a sin is a habit is not in itself a circumstance that pertains to the law of integrity. Nevertheless, a confessor may think it necessary to ask information about such a circumstance. There used to be a laxist opinion to the effect that such information is none of the confessor's business. The opinion was condemned by Pope Innocent XI. The reason for the condemnation is obvious: frequently a confessor needs to know whether a sin is habitual in order to judge the penitent's disposition or to prescribe fitting remedies for his malady.

In conclusion, let me recall that on the first Easter Sunday, when our Lord instituted the sacrament of penance, He greeted the apostles with the words, "Peace to you." Through the intervening centuries penance has indeed been a sacrament of peace. Nevertheless, it can hardly be denied that some truly good and sincere souls do not derive lasting peace from confession because they are confused about their obligation of confessing sins and tend to exaggerate these obligations. These souls in particular should be personally benefited by a knowledge of the meaning and limitations of the law of integral confession.

chapter **16**

Scruples Versus the Human Way

IN the preceding chapters I have mentioned scrupulosity several times. Everyone who gives spiritual guidance, whether to religious or to the laity, should know something of this illness: its nature, symptoms, causes, treatment. For a discussion of these points I must be content to refer the reader elsewhere.[1] In this chapter I should like to try to bring out one point: namely, how the scrupulous person differs from the ordinary person in some of the very commonplace matters of the spiritual life. My treatment may seem exaggerated; and I confess that it is exaggerated if one thinks only in terms of mild cases of scrupulosity, but I honestly doubt whether one can exaggerate the emotional struggles of severe scrupulosity.

I can best illustrate my point by speaking in terms of two imaginary characters. One of these is called

[1] See Dermot Casey, S.J., *The Nature and Treatment of Scruples* (Westminster: The Newman Press, 1948); VanderVeldt and Odenwald, *Psychiatry and Catholicism* (New York: McGraw-Hill, 1952), pp. 330-347; *Proceedings of the 1954 Sisters' Institute of Spirituality* (Notre Dame: University of Notre Dame Press, 1955), pp. 89-94.

Humanus, because he represents the ordinary conscientious human being, one who is cheerfully content to be "like the rest of men." The other character is *Scrupulosus*—so named because he typifies the victims of that gnawing and unfounded fear of sin known as scruples.

For Scrupulosus, a supreme difficulty is to appreciate what may be called "the human way of acting." It is hard to define this human way. It expresses itself in a quiet resignation to the fact that human problems cannot be solved with the exactness of mathematical problems. It is an essential requisite for peace among men and for interior peace with God and oneself.

Humanus takes this human way in full, easy stride. When a reliable man tells him something, he believes it without struggle. True, the man may be wrong, may be lying, using a mental reservation, or even deceiving himself; but Humanus does not trouble himself about these things unless there is some real evidence to make him suspect them. If a man gives him money, Humanus does not bite it or ring it on a counter. He knows the possibility of counterfeit money, but he knows too that social life demands that we practice a certain amount of trust in the good will of others.

Humanus follows the same human way in his dealings with God and himself. God made him human; God ought to be content if he simply acts humanly. And he has enough troubles in life without suspecting himself unduly.

Scrupulosus may follow the human way in his dealings with other men, but in those things which concern God and himself he is decidedly "un-human." He seems to think that, in dealing with God, he must have God's own unerring and penetrating vision of the human heart and that, in dealing with himself, none of the canons of human peace are applicable. Perhaps a few examples will make this clear.

The Sacrament of Penance

The sacrament of penance, truly a sacrament of peace according to our Lord's designs, affords no real peace to Scrupulosus. Definitely, it is a torture: a torture to go, a torture to stay away. And the reason for the torment, to put it simply, is that the reception of this sacrament involves four elements—examination of conscience, confession, contrition, satisfaction—each of which can be fulfilled only in a human way.

Suppose we follow Humanus and Scrupulosus through their preparations for confession. Humanus says a few preliminary prayers, then looks into his soul. This is not a very strenuous process for him; in fact, it verges on sheer routine. Humanus is conscious of the fact that he could improve his method, but he also knows that he fulfills all the essentials. Mortal sins first; and it does not take him long to find them. No laxist, he knows a mortal sin when he sees one; but he knows too that they are big enough to be seen with the naked eye. On some commandments he does not even examine himself. Idolatry, murder, robbing banks—all such things are off his list, and he would waste his time searching his soul for them. If he does find that he has sinned seriously, he notes the number of times; and, if he cannot recall the number, he is content to add the saving word "about." If he is doubtful concerning the serious sinfulness of anything—well, he is doubtful. There is no use wrestling with the doubt now; if he could not solve it before, he is less likely to solve it now.

Venial sins? Humanus knows there were many little things, but it is often hard to catalogue them. He selects two or three, and phrases them as best he can. Sometimes he numbers venials sins, sometimes he doesn't; and he knows that the number need not be confessed.

Finally, Humanus makes an act of contrition. In this, too, there is a trace of dry routine. Humanus has often resolved to "polish it up" a bit. Contrition never causes him worry, though it has at times puzzled him. However, he has solved the puzzle in the following manner. When a friend offends him and afterwards comes and holds out his hand and says he is sorry, Humanus takes the hand and forgives. He never looks to see if there are tears in the man's eyes. He does not stop to ask, "Now, John, are you *sure* you're sorry? Can you *swear* you're sorry? Do you *feel* sorry? Maybe you're deceiving me, or yourself?" No, Humanus does none of these things; so he solved his puzzle about contrition by deciding that God doesn't act that way, either. God is content with our just being human.

Scrupulosus also examines his conscience. After lengthy preparatory prayers, he finally musters the courage to plunge into the depths of his troubled soul. He looks for mortal sins with searchlight and microscope; and when he cannot find any, his only conclusion is that his lax conscience must be covering them up. Further examination still fails to reveal a clear mortal sin, but it does result in a sort of "doubt." This only brings the further question: "Do I really doubt?" Better to confess it as certain, because if he only thinks he is doubtful and really is not doubtful he will be deceiving the priest.

As for venial sins, he must have scores of them: morning prayers omitted, distractions in the prayers he did say, feelings he unintentionally hurt, and so on and so on. He has been told that there is no law of God or man that says we must pray in the morning; but *he* ought to pray in the morning. As for distractions, he has also been told that when involuntary they are not sinful and that even when voluntary they are merely small irreverences. But for *him* it is different; it is base ingratitude for *him* to neglect God in this manner. And the offenses—here again he knows with a rather clear speculative knowledge that an unintentional offense is not sinful; but the case is somehow different for *him*. At least, he should have foreseen that someone would be hurt by the innocent remark. And so it goes. Moreover, though he could teach others that venial sins do not have to be numbered, *he* must keep score. After all, they may be mortal sins! Well, it is time now to go to confession. He is not ready, but he will try.

For Humanus, confession follows much the same line as the preparation. He makes the confession quietly, returns to his pew and says his penance and a few prayers of devotion. The time passes very quietly. He leaves the church, full of peace and ready, as he has often expressed it, "to be hit by a truck." In a general way, he knows that his confession is not mechanically perfect. Sometimes he does not say things just as he had planned them; he becomes confused, distracted, or even a bit embarrassed. Also— and he has this on the authority of a devout priest— he knows that the confessor may become distracted or even nod a bit. But this percentage of error does not greatly concern Humanus. God Himself arranged that this sacrament should be received and administered by human beings. The essentials are quite easy to fulfill; the accidentals allow both the priest and the penitent the opportunity to strive for greater perfection and to increase in humility.

It should be evident from the story of his preparation that no great peace floods the soul of Scrupulosus as he emerges from the confessional. Nevertheless, he grits his teeth and kneels down to say his penance. Three Hail Mary's! He literally "tackles" the first one, but in the middle something goes wrong: he must have missed a word. He starts again, and then again; but he cannot satisfy himself that that Hail Mary is properly said. As he pauses in desperation, the whole blurred story of the confession begins to unfold before his mind. Nothing was said right. The priest must have misunderstood him completely. The fact that he was given only three Hail Mary's confirms him in this fear: if the priest had understood him correctly, he would have given him at least a rosary.

At this moment, a new source of interior torment

opens up. Even if the confession was good, the absolution could not be valid because he did not make a real act of contrition. He just went through some words. God must know that he was not really sorry. And his confessions have been that way for a long time . . . He simply *must* make a general confession. He has made general confessions before without any subsequent peace of soul, but *this one* will be different.

Holy Communion

We may take Holy Communion as another example of the difference between Humanus and Scrupulosus. It should be one of the supreme consolations of the Catholic's life. The essentials for its reception are very simple: the state of grace, acquired by sacramental absolution if need be; and the keeping of the fast from midnight.

Humanus finds the fulfillment of these conditions simple enough. He is satisfied with normal, human assurance that he is in the state of grace. If he doubts about a serious sin, he generally prefers to go to confession, but he knows he has no strict obligation to do so, and he is content on occasion merely to make an act of contrition and go to Communion. The fast presents no problem at all. The law is a safeguard to the reverence due the Blessed Sacrament. It forbids eating and drinking, except water, after midnight. Humanus knows what ordinary people look upon as eating and drinking, and he does not have to consult a chemist to find out just what is food or a physiologist to discover precisely what is meant by eating.

All these things are so many thorns for Scrupulosus. How does he know he is in the state of grace? He can't prove it. He is not sure he can make an act of contrition, so he must always go to confession when in doubt. It may be that his confessor has assured him again and again that, in his present trial, he may always go to Communion, no matter what his doubts, no matter how many sins he thinks he has committed. Even after this and though he knows that the providence of God guides souls through superiors and confessors, yet *his case* is different, and the confessor does not really understand it.

As for the fast, here is but one of Scrupulosus' many hard experiences with it. He is on his way to Mass. His lips tickle. He rubs his coat-sleeve over his mouth. A moment later he feels something strange in his mouth—lint from his coat, he thinks. He gathers all his salivary forces to remove it, but he is too late. He swallows. Well, that's the end. He has broken his fast; he may not go to Communion. This is his first conviction, but in church a gleam of saving common sense is still able to pierce the fog of fear and he does go to Holy Communion.

Later the fear returns with a vengeance. He made a sacrilegious Communion. After that one thing leads to another. He begins to notice a strange taste in his mouth every morning—the lint from the bedclothes! He tries again and again to remove it; but the consciousness of the lint remains, and with it the conviction that he may not receive Communion.

There are two ways of solving this lint problem. One way is to consult a trained theologian, who might show Scrupulosus by keen argumentation that lint is not food, or who might indicate that, even if it were food, it was not taken "in the manner of food." This is a perfectly legitimate method of solving the problem, but hardly a satisfactory one for Scrupulosus. It allows for too much quibbling, and, even when it does convince, its appeal is only to the intellect. Scrupulosus needs something that will impress his imagination and thus remove the emotional pressure of his fears.

The second method is therefore a much better one for Scrupulosus. It is a method suggested by an old and experienced diagnostician of this problem. It is very simple. "You take a woolly blanket, the woollier the better. Seize firmly in both hands, raise to the mouth without flinching, and bite hard. When you have a good bite, chew thoroughly *and then try to swallow.*"

This is a guaranteed cure. After one such experiment Scrupulosus needs no metaphysical discussion to be convinced that human beings do not eat coats or blankets. In this matter, at least, he will be content with *the human way.*

Chastity

Perhaps no other sphere of human life entails as much mental torture for Scrupulosus as does the practice of chastity. This is hardly surprising, because the practice of chastity demands a special blending of idealism and common sense. Though often referred to as "the angelic virtue," chastity is essentially a *human* virtue and it must be practised in a *human* way.

Before illustrating Scrupulosus' problem with chastity, it may be well to call attention to certain cases which very likely are not real scrupulosity. I refer to those cases in which, though many symptoms of scrupulosity are present, the basic difficulty is rather ignorance than fear. For instance, there are some good people who suffer from an undue anxiety regarding chastity because they really do not know what chastity is. At some time in their lives they developed the notion that chastity includes just about everything pertaining to the discipline of the senses and the affections; and, because of this erroneous widening of the scope of chastity, they are unnecessarily fearful of violating the virtue. This type of worry can be dispelled by the simple process of obtaining correct information as to the meaning of chastity.

Other good people know, at least in a general way, the scope of chastity, but do not know the difference between temptation and sin in this matter. Such people are ignorant of the simple principle that *what is not wilful cannot be sinful.* They are prone to brand "sinful," imaginations and feelings that are no more wilful than a shudder or the blink of an eyelash. They set themselves to do the impossible—that is, to exclude even spontaneous sense impulses; and, when they have failed to do this, they think they have sinned. The obvious result is discouragement, worry, fear; the obvious remedy is instruction.

Our genuine Scrupulosus knows the meaning of chastity and of sin. In fact, he may have even a superior degree of *theoretical* knowledge; but he is *afraid* to apply it practically to himself. Fear enslaves him and paralyzes his judgment. He does not trust himself; he cannot, or will not, put his confidence in God.

That is the general analysis of Scrupulosus' problem. But to make it more concrete it may be helpful to continue the contrast between him and Humanus as regards some of the normal problems of chastity.

Take the question of "bad thoughts." Both Humanus and Scrupulosus are subject to them, and each has characteristic reactions to them. Humanus knows, of course, that disturbing imaginations can come unbidden into the mind and that they are often accompanied by tempting feelings and impulses. Nevertheless, though not imprudent, he is not afraid of them nor perpetually on the lookout for them. When they do pass through his mind, he ignores them. Even when they persist and grow strong, he is usually content with the quiet judgment, "I don't want these things," a short aspiration for grace, and a sincere, calm attempt to think of other things. Occasionally he may find it advisable to read a book to distract himself. Now and then he even has doubts about his guilt; but these doubts are not a source of worry for him. He knows this is a human problem, and he deals with it the human way.

Unlike Humanus, Scrupulosus is afraid of bad thoughts. When he hasn't any, he is afraid that he will have them; and this makes him more susceptible to them. When they do come, his fear that he will give in to them incites him to engage them immediately in an interior wrestling match instead of resorting to the much more salutary method of ignoring them.

It is a wrestling match that seldom results in a complete victory for Scrupulosus. His common sense tries to draw him away with the quiet, cheery message: "Don't bother about these things. If you let them alone they won't hurt you. Remember, it's not your fault they're here. Involuntary things are never sinful."

But the voice of his fear, louder and sharper than that of common sense, goads him on. "That's just the point," argues fear. "*Are* they involuntary? They're pleasant, aren't they? Maybe you do want them! Maybe you did something that brought them on! Maybe they're the result of your other sins! And even if you don't want them now, maybe you will want them. You'd better act fast. You'd better pitch them out right now, or you'll be guilty of mortal sin."

Blinded by fear, Scrupulous ignores the voice of common sense. He tries to shake the thoughts out of his head; he clenches his fists; he prays desperately. He keeps his nerves at bowstring tautness, so that fear can play its haunting challenge on them. And when the temptation is over—for a while—he looks back on it with the eyes of fear. He dare not decide that he didn't sin; yet he's not sure that he did. Then he's not sure that he isn't sure; and in the end he succumbs, not to a judgment, but to a despairing conviction dictated by fear: "I guess I must have sinned!"

The foregoing are more or less typical reactions to

involuntary and unforeseen thoughts and feelings. Another problem concerns voluntary thoughts and actions that are good in themselves but which are quite likely to be accompanied by temptations against chastity. There are many such thoughts and actions: for example, the study of the sixth commandment, the study of physiology, normal social dealings with certain attractive persons, the care of the sick, the care of one's own body, reading that contains suggestive descriptions, and so forth. Many people know from experience that such things as these are apt to excite impulses and feelings that would be unchaste if deliberately indulged in. Hence arises the problem whether all such thoughts and actions must be avoided?

For determining whether any deliberate action or line of thought that is likely to result in physical disturbances and temptations against chastity is permissible, the following set of questions is simple, yet scientifically sound: (1) Is the *action* itself impure? If so, it is wrong; if not, the remaining questions are applicable. (2) Is my *motive* impure; that is, am I seeking to arouse passion or trying to lead to an impure action? (3) Have I *a reasonable assurance of preserving self-control* if I should be tempted? (4) Have I a *relatively sufficient reason* for this particular action or line of thought—in other words, is the good to be accomplished of sufficient value to justify my tolerating the physical reactions and temptation?

For example, consider the case of one who needs instruction concerning chastity. It may be that the instruction itself, at least in the beginning, will be a source of disquiet to him. Foreseeing this difficulty, he can satisfy the demands of conscience by applying the four questions to his problem.

The application might run somewhat as follows: (1) *The action?* Certainly the study of chastity is not wrong in itself; otherwise not even priests could study or give information. (2) *The motive?* In this case the purpose is to obtain useful, even necessary, information, and the eventual peace of mind that comes with it. The evil effects accompanying the study are merely tolerated. (3) *Self-control?* This is a personal problem; yet the normal good person who is not accustomed to sin against chastity and who is willing to take the ordinary means of safeguarding his will against temptation usually has a reasonable assurance on this point. (4) *Sufficient Reason?* Such reasons are relative, depending on the degree of the disturbance and the force of the temptation. In this case, since the information is really useful, even necessary, it constitutes a sufficient reason for tolerating even strong physical reactions and temptations.

The first of the questions would seldom present serious difficulty to anyone who is well instructed as to the meaning of chastity, though, of course, it is the great stumbling-block for the ignorant. But it is well to note that the other three questions can rarely be answered with perfect exactness. They carry us definitely into the *human* sphere; they involve delicate subjective elements and the weighing of rather intangible pros and cons. Most people have to be content with answering these according to a "rough estimate."

Humanus doesn't mind rough estimates. He makes

them often in all spheres of life. Why should he demand more in the matter of chastity? Suppose, for
instance, that his work calls for the reading of a book
that he knows will be a source of some disturbance
to him. His motive? Well, he knows he might deceive himself; yet he is not conscious of any impure
motive or self-deception now, and he does have a
rather obvious good purpose. Hence he concludes
that his motive is good. His self-control? Yes, he has
occasionally lost self-control in temptation, but it
was only occasional, and he now has what appears to
be a prudent confidence that he can control himself;
so he doesn't worry about that point. Does the good
outweigh the evil? Humanus knows that he cannot
put the good effects of his action on one side of a
scale and the evil effects on the other; but he also
knows that the reading is necessary, or at least definitely useful for his work, and his good sense tells
him that this outweighs merely unintentional physical reactions and temptations. Life is seldom all
white; a bit of black must often be tolerated.

Scrupulosus detests rough estimates. Each of the
last three questions affords his fear a veritable field
day.

"How do you know you have a good motive? Lots
of people act from hidden impure motives. You yourself have had evil motives before. You're just trying
to cover up your guilt so that you can enjoy yourself.

"As for self-control, haven't you lost it before?
Even if your motive were good now, how could you
know you wouldn't weaken? This temptation may be
especially strong. Remember what the Scripture says
about the man who thinketh himself to stand. You're

putting yourself in the proximate occasion of sin right now; and that means you're already sinning.

"Good and evil! How can you balance good and evil? A little bit of evil outweighs a vast amount of good. Furthermore, how do you know this reading is useful or necessary? You don't really need it. You could get along without it. It's easy to deceive yourself into thinking things are necessary or useful when pleasure is connected with them. That's what you're doing now—deceiving yourself. Then you'll go to confession and deceive your confessor. But remember: *you can't deceive God!*"

The second struggle ends in the same manner as the first—with Scrupulosus a beaten man. If he does the things he has a perfect right to do, his fear continues to plague him, especially with the taunt that he is acting "against his conscience"; if he does not do these things, he is deprived of many useful, even necessary, benefits of normal human living. And even then he is not at peace.

The result of these interior conflicts is often a profound discouragement. Scrupulosus may begin to look upon chastity as something impossible for him, and this leads to the very real danger that he will cease to care whether he practices it. His scruples, unlike a truly delicate conscience, become the worst enemy to his chastity.

Conclusion

No one should judge from this brief series of contrasts between Humanus and Scrupulosus that the latter does not wish to act as others do. His difficulty is more profound. Briefly put, it seems to be this: he has not learned the secret of relaxing interiorly. At times he is like the sick man who fights an anesthetic; at other times he resembles the man who *will* take the anesthetic even if it kills him. Thus Scrupulosus sometimes fights his fears, while at other times he clenches his fists and insists that he *will* ignore them. In both cases there is tension, and fear thrives on tension.

But how relax? It is not easy. But some things help. For instance, there is the cultivation of a child-like trust in God. Scrupulosus needs this. A child-like attitude towards God brings about an interior relaxation just as—if I may pursue the metaphor— physical childhood is endowed with exterior relaxation. Note how easily the small boy wiggles under a fence when the stiff-jointed adult is almost sure to get caught on something.

It also helps for Scrupulosus to cultivate the power of seeing the absurdity of his frantic efforts to be absolutely certain of things. A good laugh is wonderfully relaxing; and Scrupulosus must learn to laugh at himself. In fact, for him, a sense of humor is far more precious than the gift of tears.

chapter 17

How to Think and Act
About the Race Problem

THE title of this chapter was suggested by two pamphlets: *How to Think about Race,* by Louis J. Twomey, S.J., and *Fifty Ways to Improve Race Relations,* by Frank A. Riley.[1] The word "problem" is not in either pamphlet title, but the fact of a problem is very much in both authors' minds; they wrote their pamphlets to help solve a problem. Both pamphlets refer explicitly to the Negro problem, but their content applies equally to the problem of discrimination against other minorities, such as the Mexicans, the Japanese, the Chinese, and so forth. My remarks will also be directed to the Negro problem, but they too can be applied to the other problems.

The Problem

In thinking about the race problem, the first thing to do is to recognize that there is a problem. Some people believe—or would like to believe—that there is no problem. When you mention the Negro prob-

[1] Both pamphlets were published by The Queen's Work, St. Louis, Missouri.

lem to them, they look puzzled, raise their eyebrows a bit, and ask icily, "*Is* there a Negro problem?" Others admit the problem, but explain it very simply by saying: "There would be no problem if the Negro would keep his place." (These, incidentally, do not say "Negro.")

No unbiassed and even moderately well-informed person can fail to see that we have a race problem— or, to be more specific, a Negro problem. And it consists, not in the fact that the Negro will not keep his place, but rather in the fact that white people will not let him have his place. The two-volume work *An American Dilemma*, by Gunnar Myrdal, is a scholarly, factual proof of the existence of the problem. And hundreds of books, pamphlets, and articles that have appeared within the last decade or two give further evidence not only of the existence but of the magnitude of the problem.

To see that we have a Negro problem, one has but to consider what ought to be and what is the status of the Negro in the United States. There is always a problem when the *is* falls below the *ought to be*. There is a problem in our personal spiritual lives when our conduct falls short of our standards; there is a problem in our social order when the income of the working man is not what it should be; and there is a problem in millions of personal lives and in the social order of the nation when an entire race is daily accorded a treatment that is contrary to the laws of God and of the nation.

What *ought to be* the status of the Negro? Like other men, he has a human nature and he is destined, through the providence of God, for heaven. This common nature and common destiny should *unite* men. By reason of their common nature and common destiny they are one family. This unity is expressed through love in the natural order, and through charity in the supernatural order. And love (charity) expresses itself through kindly thoughts, prayers for one another, words of courtesy, cooperation, and mutual help. This bond of love joins all men; the commandment of love knows no distinction of race.

Like other men, the Negro is a human person, a distinct individual; and by reason of his human personality he is the subject not only of duties but of inviolable rights. He has the same right as other men to say "mine," and to have what is his respected by other men. He has the same right as others to worship God. He has a right to life and liberty as long as he is not proved guilty of crime. He has a right to equality of opportunity to make a decent living, to develop his talents, to marry and provide for his family, to enjoy recreational facilities, to have his share of honor. These rights, conferred by God, are confirmed by the law of the nation when it makes the Negro an American citizen. And to these rights, the nation either adds civil rights or guarantees equality of opportunity in obtaining such civil rights.

What *is* the status of the Negro in the United States? He is segregated—forced to live apart from the white men—and thus the law of union is violated; he is discriminated against—treated as an inferior—and thus the law of equality is violated. His life is less secure than the white man's; he has less opportunity to obtain the necessities and comforts of life. He is more readily arrested and more easily convicted. On one streetcar he finds a sign, "This space reserved for our colored patrons"; on another, where no printed sign is displayed, he finds "Unwelcome" written on white faces. While traveling he has difficulty securing proper accommodations and even obtaining food. He must say "sir" to the white man, but he is called, "Johnny," "Doc," or "Uncle." His house is a menace to his physical well-being, and his congested surroundings are a greater menace to his soul's welfare. When he tries to move to another neighborhood, he is repelled by violence, thwarted by restrictive covenants, or humiliated by the exodus of prospective white neighbors who flee him as they would a contagion. He sees his children denied educational opportunities, his wife and mother denied the courtesies extended to other women. Even in his worship, he must have a "special" church or a "special" place in the white man's church.

These and scores of other insults, humiliations, frustrations, are the daily fare of the American Negro. Not that all the abuses are practiced everywhere and by everyone; but the general pattern is so common, even in the North, that some unprejudiced scholars do not hesitate to call it our greatest national scandal. It is not an accidental pattern; it is a calculated system of oppression and contempt.

Perhaps the scholars just referred to were not conscious of the theological meaning of "scandal," but Catholics should be definitely conscious of it. Theologically, scandal is an occasion of spiritual harm to the neighbor. Scandal is very seriously involved when white Catholics practice racial segregation and discrimination, because their conduct makes it very difficult for Negro Catholics to preserve the faith and well-nigh impossible to convert Negroes to the faith. There can scarcely be greater scandal than this.

From what I have written (which is just a brief repetition of what has been said and written often and more forcefully by others) it should be evident that we have a problem. Despite the fact that recent years have witnessed a strong trend against discrimination and some improvement in the status of the Negro, his condition is still not what it ought to be. He is still the victim of a policy which was described in a report issued by the Sacred Congregation for the Propagation of the Faith as a "grave derogation to the Christian concept of the individual's inherent dignity." [2] This policy involves contempt, hatred, and scandal. And the responsibility lies, not with the Negro victim, but with the white people who either willingly perpetuate the policy or negligently refuse to do what they can to stop it.

How to think about the Negro problem? I said that the first thing to do is to recognize the problem. The second is suggested by another statement in the report of the Sacred Congregation for the Propagation of the Faith. The report says that the "thought

[2] The report, printed in pamphlet form under the title *The Catholic Church and Negroes in the United States,* can be obtained from the Catholic Interracial Council of Chicago, 21 West Superior Street, Chicago 10, Illinois.

of a widespread, general conversion of the Negroes to the Catholic Church is an illusion until and unless the attitude of American Catholics—clergy and laity —*is completely purified of approval of the segregation policy* or of the many deprivations of educational opportunity, of fair employment, and of decent housing that arise as a result of it." The words I have italicized indicate the second step in thinking correctly about the Negro problem: We must *disapprove* of the segregation policy, which is, in fact, a colossal violation of justice and charity. Such disapproval, incidentally, is not a counsel of perfection; it is a strict duty, and a serious one.

What to Do

An evil is not removed by recognizing its existence. Something constructive has to be done. "But," an individual will say, "I am so small, and this evil is so great and so widespread. How can I do anything about it?" Actually, there is much that any individual white person of good will can do regarding the Negro problem; and it is my purpose, taking a cue from Mr. Riley's pamphlet, to indicate some of these things here. It may be noted that much of what I say seems to have no special pertinence to religious. Yet it does pertain to religious, as well as to other people, and in one sense at least it has a special application to religious, because religious by reason of their position in the Church have an influence for good or bad that is altogether special.

A constructive solution to the Negro problem must work "from the inside out." I mean that it must begin with correct attitudes, with an inner spirit that

[308]

will be the soul of external action. Vast numbers of
people do not have this inner spirit. As François
Mauriac states forcefully in his *Life of Jesus,* at the
conclusion of the chapter on the Samaritan woman:

> He tarried for two days in the midst of the outcast
> Samaritans, thus giving his followers an example
> which was to be transmitted in vain to the rest of the
> world. For if there is a part of the Christian message
> which men have refused and rejected with invincible
> obstinacy, it is faith in the equal value of all souls, of
> all races, before the Father who is in heaven.

The indictment is dreadfully true, but it does not
make our case hopeless. Even the devil of racial
hatred must yield to prayer and self-sacrifice. That is
why *Fifty Ways of Improving Race Relations* insists
much on the need of prayer, of prayer "that light
may shine in dark areas of white men's minds, that
the race heresy may be put down." Any one of us has
this power of prayer, and we can use it to beg for
ourselves and others a vital appreciation of the truths
of reason and faith that are the foundation of racial
amity and justice.

Many white people, it is said, are not malicious;
they simply have such an aversion for the Negro that
they abhor the very thought of living with him on
equal terms. I admit the existence of this psychological problem. Yet it seems to me that it can be and is
overrated. It is not substantially different from the
problem of aversion as sometimes experienced by one
white person towards another, even by one religious
towards another. Morally speaking, the aversion itself is merely a feeling, and as such it is not culpable.
Nevertheless, since the fostering of this feeling can

be the source of great harm, it must be disciplined like other dangerous emotions, and proper means must be taken to eliminate or to temper it. And here again a first remedy is prayer. It should not be too much for anyone to ask sincerely for the grace to act according to Christian principles, despite a feeling of antipathy. After all, we do this regularly when we pray for the grace to preserve chastity, despite strong contrary feelings.

Many students of the race problem say that aversion to the Negro springs from ignorance and that it disappears or subsides when one gets to know the Negro. Some white people who have lived near Negroes for many years might answer this by saying that no one knows the Negro better than they, yet their knowledge has not affected their aversion. I think that one might legitimately question whether such people really know the Negro. Real knowledge of a person implies something more than just being near him. Real knowledge comes in friendship, from getting under the surface into a man's heart and his feelings. The system of segregation and discrimination is itself a block to such knowledge, and it perpetuates a vicious circle by which aversion fosters segregation and segregation fosters aversion.

More than twenty years ago Father Francis J. Gilligan wrote in *The Morality of the Color Line*: [3]

To be forced always to seek a restaurant on the rear street, to be placed always at a table in some alcove, to be compelled always to accept a seat in the gallery

[3] This book is out of print. It is a real pioneer study—and a very capable one—of race relations in the light of Christian moral prin-

of a theatre, to be denied access to every respectable and standard hotel, or be driven constantly to tax one's ingenuity to secure a reservation in a Pullman, are conditions which would occasion in every man, and the Negro is no exception, anger and despair. A white person probably can never fully realize the anxiety and hesitancy which the Negro experiences almost daily in trying to satisfy conventional needs.

Father Gilligan is undoubtedly correct when he says that probably a white man can never *fully* appreciate what the Negro experiences. Nevertheless, any white man with good will and a good imagination can learn much by using what psychologists call "empathy"—namely, by putting himself in the Negro's place, by trying to feel what the Negro feels in the various frustrating circumstances that make up the pattern of discrimination. Psychologically, this cultivation of a strong "fellow-feeling" is perhaps the best antidote for aversion, because one powerful emotion tends to neutralize the other. Besides, deep feeling for the Negro stimulates constructive action in his behalf. Some of the greatest strides towards interracial justice have been made by white men who had the power of sharing the hurt feelings of the Negro.

To stimulate this fellow-feeling, it helps to read a good autobiography, like *Dark Symphony,* by Elizabeth Adams. For the same purpose—but to a lesser

ciples. Father Gilligan is professor of moral theology at The St. Paul Seminary, St. Paul, Minnesota. He has for many years been Chairman of the Governor's Interracial Commission of Minnesota, a commission that has done very constructive work in the matter of race relations and that has published some splendid leaflets and booklets.

degree, because the personal element is wanting—it is useful to get a complete picture of the wrongs done the Negro by reading *An American Dilemma* (or at least the condensation of this work, entitled *The Negro in America* by Arnold Rose, one of Myrdal's collaborators). I would not recommend these two works, however, without adding the caution that their otherwise scientific and morally wholesome tone is marred by the section that recommends artificial birth-control as a means of solving the problem of "Negro overpopulation." (See Myrdal, I, 175-181; Rose, 60-61.)

Before I leave the subject of aversion, I should like to add that the white man has no monopoly on it. The Negro too has an aversion for the white man— and understandably so, in view of what he has suffered. But, like the white man, he must be willing to put aside or temper this aversion in order to establish a Christian system of race relations. I am not stressing this here because my main concern is with indicating things that white people can and should do as regards the Negro.

From the inside to the outside—that is, from thoughts and feelings to words and actions. A prime rule of speech is to avoid what reasonably offends other people. On the basis of this rule, a Negro should not be called a "nigger," and a Negro woman should not be referred to as a "negress." Both words are offensive to Negroes, as are many others that need not be mentioned here. The best way for anyone to keep this rule is to abstain entirely from using the words because, if white people use them among themselves when speaking about the Negro, they very readily use them when speaking to the Negro. Another basic rule of speech is to be extremely careful about repeating unverified and disparaging rumors about the Negro. "Seldom in the history of mankind," wrote Father Gilligan, "has any group been more widely misrepresented, misunderstood, and handicapped by popular rumors than the American colored group." Accepting such unfounded rumors is rash judgment; passing them on to others is calumny.

As regards both speech and conduct, I should like to stress one point that is of particular interest to the moral theologian. In our theological treatises on the virtue of charity, as I pointed out in a preceding chapter, we make much of what are called the common signs of good will and courtesy. These are various little gestures and words that are due to all fellow citizens, fellow workers, neighbors, and the like, and not merely to one's special friends. I think it is very important that every individual white person be conscious of this duty when he is dealing with Negroes. If he says "sir" to a white man, he should say "sir" to a Negro; if he tips his hat to a white woman, he should also tip his hat to a Negro woman; if he says "good morning" to white neighbors, he should say "good morning" to his Negro neighbors; if he shakes hands with a white person to whom he is introduced, he should shake hands with a Negro under the same circumstances. In themselves these are small things, and any individual with good will can do them; yet failure to use them can cause deep hurt

[313]

and humiliation, whereas their use can cause genuine elation to those who have been constantly denied them. Moreover, they manifest just what is needed to improve race relations: good will and respect.

The foregoing are ways in which any white individual can help to improve race relations, even though others do not cooperate with him. But for any grand-scale reformation of the social order, there must be group action, as our recent popes have stated so often. *Fifty Ways to Improve Race Relations* contains many suggestions for participation in group action: for example, by helping such organizations as the National Association for the Advancement of Colored People, the Urban League, various interracial councils; by voting for good social legislation, by joining with others to urge congressmen to promote such legislation, by signing petitions to have Negroes admitted to schools that make a policy of excluding them, by joining in protests to owners of stores, restaurants, and hotels which discriminate against Negroes. By these and various other ways the apparent insignificance of the individual can become a very significant force in establishing a Christian social order in our race relations.

Special for Religious

In themselves these points, as I mentioned previously, have no special pertinence to us as religious. Yet, since they pertain to all persons of good will, they certainly pertain to us too; and we can and should carry them out in our personal lives. Moreover, they have a very special pertinence to us be-

cause of our position of leadership among Catholics:
we are expected to teach Catholic doctrine by word
and example—and, one might say, particularly by example. The best argument against segregated schools
is to have our own schools unsegregated; the best
way to denounce segregation in worship is to have
no color line in our own churches and chapels; and
the best way to condemn discrimination in profes-
sions is to have our own convents and seminaries wide
open to all qualified applicants, irrespective of race.
And certainly the best—if not the only—way to in-
spire youth to practice justice and charity is to be
gracious exemplars of these virtues in our own daily
lives.

The effects, good or bad, of even our smallest public actions are tremendous. *The Priest* for May, 1951,
published an article entitled "Black Priest," which
contains the reflections of a Negro convert studying
for the priesthood. Two incidents recounted in the
article indicate the effects of even our small actions.
On one occasion, when the author had returned to
his home in the South for the funeral of an aunt, two
white women, one of them a nun, came to visit him.
On another occasion, while he was driving with some
of his colored friends, he stopped to visit a monastery,
and the superior insisted that he bring his friends in
and treated them with true monastic hospitality.
These courtesies had a profoundly salutary effect on
his friends, helping them to see that the Catholic
Church is not "a white man's church."

"These incidents," reflects the author, "may seem
like little things, but what if that good sister and

other lady had not come to see me? What if we had been turned away from the door of the monastery? For one thing, I probably would have kept the promise I made to myself never to go South again. But the most serious result would have been that more souls would have been pushed farther and farther away from the Church. Those were two times when I was really proud of my fellow Catholics. May God bless them!"

Index

[317]

A NOTE ON THE TYPE

IN WHICH THIS BOOK IS SET

This book is set in Baskerville, a Linotype face, created from the original types used by John Baskerville, the eighteenth-century typefounder and printer. This type has long been considered one of the finest book types ever developed. The letters are wide and open and have a businesslike approach. The finer hairlines give exquisite delicacy. The heavier strokes give color and strength. The relation of the two in combination gives a brilliant effect and makes for easy reading. The book was composed and printed by the Wickersham Printing Company of Lancaster, Pa., and bound by Moore and Company of Baltimore. The typography and design are by Howard N. King.